Reflections from Canoe Country

Ampersand Brook in the shadow of Stony Creek Mountain.

Reflections from Canoe Country

Paddling the Waters of the Adirondacks and Canada

Christopher Angus

With a Foreword by Paul Jamieson
Drawings by Anna Gerhard Arnold

Syracuse University Press

Copyright © 1997 by Syracuse University Press
Syracuse, New York 13244-5160
All Rights Reserved

First Edition 1997
97 98 99 00 01 02   6 5 4 3 2 1

This book is published with the assistance of a grant
from the John Ben Snow Foundation.

The paper used in this publication meets the minimum requirements
of American National Standard for Information Sciences—Permanence
of Paper for Printed Library Materials, ANSI Z39.48-1984. ♾™

Library of Congress Cataloging-in-Publication Data
Angus, Christopher.
Reflections from canoe country : paddling the waters of the
Adirondacks and Canada / Christopher Angus ; with a foreword by Paul
Jamieson ; drawings by Anna Gerhard Arnold. — 1st ed.
p.   cm.
ISBN 0-8156-0444-0 (cloth : alk. paper)
1. Adirondack Mountains (N.Y.)—Description and travel.
2. Canada, Eastern—Description and travel.   3. Canoes and canoeing—
New York (State)—Adirondack Mountains.   4. Canoes and canoeing—
Canada, Eastern.   I. Title.
F127.A2A2757   1997
917.47'50443—dc21   97-4281

Manufactured in the United States of America

For Kathy

Christopher Angus is book review editor for *Adirondac* magazine and has, for many years, written a weekly column for the *St. Lawrence Plaindealer* and the *Advance News*. He has been involved in lobbying for the passage of the Environmental Protection Act and in efforts to reopen Adirondack rivers to the public.

The river flows. The river will not wait.

—EDWARD ABBEY

Contents

Politics

Perspectives

Canada

Illustrations

Foreword

PAUL JAMIESON

In June of 1986 three indignant canoeists knocked at my door. They had been ticketed and fined for alleged trespass on an Adirondack river claimed private by the hunting club that leased thousands of acres from a timber company. As writer of a guide to canoeing on Adirondack waters, I was interested in their story. For several years I had campaigned to open to public navigation sections of Adirondack rivers (in two instances, entire rivers) that had been posted for up to a century. I held that in common law there is a public easement on all rivers navigable in fact.

Christopher Angus was spokesman for the trio. He told with precision, thoroughness, and humor the circumstances of the ticketing in a remote area and of the summary pronouncement of guilt by a rustic justice of the peace in a tiny office of the town barn. Chris was inclined to appeal the conviction to county court. I encouraged him to do so, hoping for a comprehensive ruling about public rights. The conviction was in fact overturned but on the narrowest possible ground of failure to prove beyond doubt that the three paddlers had trespassed on private land in egress from the river at a bridge on a public road.

Outrage over the original conviction and fine was one of the motives that launched Chris Angus as columnist in two of the Park newspapers of St. Lawrence County. *Canoe Country* was the heading he chose. For him canoe country comprised the Adirondacks (his lifelong home being just off the northwest corner of the park) and much of Canada, home of his ancestors and frequent goal of his vacations. For several years I have been a regular reader and admirer of this column, and I finally suggested he might make a book of it.

No devotee of the late E. B. White can belittle the column as a literary type. White himself once remarked about a fellow columnist: "One out of every three things he writes is very good, which isn't a bad average." When a columnist compiles a book and, as Angus has done, adds new pieces written expressly for the book, he improves on that average by discarding his failures.

Angus probes the timeless aspects of a columnist's timely topics. His writing is concise as limitation of space obliges and yet intimate enough to project personality. It is also diverse in its exploration of a wide range of canoe country and its evocation of a paddler's pleasures and apprehensions over the possible loss of the wild places he loves. The piece "Perceptions" is a key to his best writing: awareness of the surroundings.

Montaigne paired the adjectives "undulant and diverse" to describe the new man of the awakening that succeeded the somnolent Middle Age. They seem to fit here. Reading these short pieces in rhythmic sequence is like riding the waves in a kayak off the Nova Scotia coast, as Angus likes to do.

Acknowledgments

This work is dedicated to my wife, Kathy, who has for so long encouraged and supported my twin passions, paddling and writing. If not for her gift to me of my first computer, this book would never have appeared.

To my parents, Douglas and Sylvia Angus, I owe nothing less than my ability to put words together in a way that "works." I grew up in a household full of writers, and there can be little doubt as to their collective impact. One of them, my sister Jamie, has been editor and booster for so long that her name might more appropriately appear on the cover. And to my daughter, Emma, I owe inspiration, for which I need only look into her eyes.

If not for the discovery of my paddling soul mate of the past two decades, Jim Smith, I would probably still be lost somewhere on the Grass River. Jim's love for paddling, his good companionship and his ability to master so many skills that have long escaped me, have made my back country experiences immeasurably more pleasant. If not for his desire to "push the envelope," the pieces on sea kayaking here would never have been written.

My debt to Paul Jamieson is profound. It was with his encouragement that I published "Busted on the Banks," thus beginning this odyssey. He has continued to provide support, editorial comment, and even the occasional loan of his kevlar canoe, not to mention the foreword herein. Such good-natured support is nothing new for Paul. He has done the same for countless writers. My thanks and indeed the thanks of all paddlers should be tendered to Paul for his tireless efforts to retrieve the once posted and forbidden rivers of the Adirondack Park for this and future generations.

A large measure of gratitude goes to Neal Burdick, editor of *Adirondac,* for his support and for the opportunity to write for one of the best small publications in the country, in no small measure due to Neal's long tenure there. My thanks also to David Trithart for his research and computer skills but mostly for his refusal ten years ago to let his two canoeing partners accept, without protest, a trespassing ticket on the South Branch of the Grass River.

I owe a debt to Richard Beamish for the invitation to go paddling with a legend that resulted in the piece "Day Trip." And another to one of my oldest friends, he of the recently difficult initials to own up to, O. J. Audet, who single-handedly brought me, kicking and screaming all the way, into the computer age.

My thanks to *Adirondac* for permission to reprint "Bringing Back the Moose," "Awakening," and "Long Lake Revisited," to *Adirondack Life* for the use of "Busted on the Banks," written with the help of David Trithart, and to John Turcotte and Charles Kelly for the opportunity to write for the *St. Lawrence Plaindealer* and the *Advance News.*

Finally, my deep appreciation to Anna Gerhard Arnold, whose inspired illustrations of the North Country have made this work more beautiful than I could have hoped.

CHRISTOPHER ANGUS

Canton, New York

Watersheds

To cherish we must see and fondle, and when enough have seen and fondled, there is no wilderness left to cherish.

—ALDO LEOPOLD

Beyond Sunday Rock

Just outside the tiny village of South Colton in the northwest corner of the Adirondack Mountains of New York State sits a large glacial erratic that has come to be known as Sunday Rock. To generations of loggers, river drivers, fishermen, hunters, college students, and schoolchildren, this rock has long been a symbol of the boundary between civilization and the land of the deep North Woods. Beyond this stone, it was said, there was no Sunday. The rules of man no longer applied.

How far back the legend of Sunday Rock goes, no one knows. But the value of the great wilderness it defines was recognized early on. Since 1885, much of the land beyond Sunday Rock has been protected and, since 1894, declared "forever wild" by the constitution of the state of New York. That land is known today as the Adirondack Park.

I live just a few miles north of Sunday Rock. I have passed it at the start of hundreds of trips into the woods to canoe, camp, ski, and hike. But on this day, as I pass the rock, my mind is on a very different mission.

It is early June, a Currier and Ives day. Puffy white clouds scud rapidly across the heavens, chased by a brisk spring breeze. I speed down familiar Route 56 to Sevey's Corners and turn onto Route 3, which connects Cranberry Lake with Tupper Lake. It is a good road now, the legacy of much Department of Transportation work leading up to the 1980 Winter Olympics in Lake Placid. People like the roads. Most of the other legacies of the games are not so admired, especially by the old-timers who can remember when Lake Placid was still a sleepy wilderness town, back before the other Olympics held here in 1932.

3

Adirondack wilderness with Lake Placid alterations.

Today, Lake Placid resembles a sort of shrunken Miami Beach. There is only one main street and the entire distance from one end to the other is hardly more than a mile. But what a mile: many huge motels and hotels march along the route, Ramada, Hilton, Best Western, Holiday Inn, and, a bit incongruously, St. Moritz. An old-timer might well shake his head as he strolls down a main street now lined with antique dealers, art galleries, boutiques, discotheques, health spas, tanning salons, and rare book dealers. There are numerous ski, mountaineer, hiking, camping, and canoeing rental and equipment suppliers. And then there are the Olympic buildings themselves, the ice skating oval where Eric Heiden did his thing to the tune of five golden medals and the hockey arena where U.S. skaters stunned an overconfident Russian team. Towering over it all is the huge ski-jump facility, nestling in the clouds, seemingly aloof, finally, to the contentious debate that flared around its construction.

The once-majestic Lake Placid Club hovers in the distance on the shores of Mirror Lake. A few years ago, the famous old resort flirted with resurrection. The Gleneagles Corporation of Great Britain announced that they would create a massive, world-class resort, complete with hundreds of new rooms, suburbs of condominiums, riding stables, tennis courts, and two eighteen-hole golf courses designed by Arnold Palmer. The plans were met with astounded huzzahs by businessmen and developers. But others questioned the wisdom of such an enormous expansion. What of traffic congestion, lost mountain vistas, inadequate sewage and water facilities, rising property taxes—how on earth could that single main street handle an influx of thousands of additional people? The project languished as impact statement followed impact statement until finally the recession of 1990–92—George Bush's recession—forced Gleneagles to cancel the entire project.

But Lake Placid is not on my route or my mind today. From Tupper Lake I take the road to Long Lake, Blue Mountain Lake, and Raquette Lake. There are so many lakes, some twenty-seven hundred of them in this park along with an estimated thirty thousand miles of rivers and streams. They are the real reason I have come to love this place, for it is quite simply one of the best spots in the world for canoeing.

The road from Tupper Lake to Long Lake is twenty-two miles in length, and as I drive along, I reflect on how unusual a road it is, every mile so magnificently free of roadside advertising. The Adirondack Sign Law of 1924 is the reason. Ahead of its time, it was one of the earliest private land use control laws based on aesthetics. It resulted in the removal of over fourteen hundred signs. The law remains on the books today virtually unchanged from its original form, a lasting tribute to what can be achieved if only a few of the people can be aroused.

At Long Lake, I pull over near the bridge that spans the fourteen-mile-long body of water. I stare out at the foaming whitecaps that the strong breeze has whipped up. In the distance is a fully loaded canoe, and I watch as its two stalwarts paddle doggedly against the wind. I have been where they are now, many times. I can almost feel the ache that throbs between their shoulders and the fire of muscles straining for hours. Yet I wish grimly that I was with them rather than where I am heading, even though, when they at last reach the lean-tos at the foot of the lake, they will undoubtedly find them taken. Even though they will have to make a rough camp on a brushy shore. Even though the black flies will be upon them by the thousands before they have pulled their canoe high enough to begin unloading it.

That's how much I want not to be going where I am going.

Speaking in front of a crowd is not my favorite way to spend a beautiful spring evening. Public speaking of any kind ranks first among phobias of most Americans, and I have had very little experience in it. Yet, as I drive through this park, I feel my resolve hardening. For despite the beautiful day, despite even that landmark sign law, this is not the same park that I drove through as a boy or even as a young man.

It has changed, and I know the reasons why only too well. In the past twenty years, the number of dwellings in the Adirondack Park increased by more than 40 percent. There are twenty thousand new homes on roadsides and lakeshores, around villages, and in formerly undisturbed backcountry. For years, the state had no funds to purchase threatened lands or even easements. The Adirondack Park Agency, the sole control over development run rampant, is severely underbudgeted and overworked. Large tracts of wilderness that have been offered for sale to the state are in danger of being auctioned off to the highest bidder.

At risk is the Follensby Pond Tract, more than fourteen thousand acres adjoining the High Peaks Wilderness Area and bordering the exquisite canoeing of the Raquette River. The pond was the site in 1858 of the famous Philosophers' Camp, where Ralph Waldo Emerson, James Russell Lowell, William J. Stillman, and others camped and where today there remain over ten miles of undisturbed shoreline.

At risk is the incomparable Whitney estate, fifty-one thousand forested acres that include some forty undisturbed lakes in the heart of the Adirondacks. Its purchase would open up new canoe routes along many miles of rivers and lakes that were once enjoyed by tourists more than a hundred years ago, but that have since been lost because of posting.

At risk are miles of untouched shoreline along Lake Champlain, the lower Raquette River, Lake George, and the Hudson River Gorge. The list goes on and on and the developers want it all.

Not just some of it. They want it all. During a recent session of the legislature, Senate majority leader Ronald Stafford introduced a bill that would have eliminated the Adirondack Park Agency completely, thus opening up more than half the park to uncontrolled development. Stafford was also credited with single-handedly halting passage of legislation to protect the park. As a senator whose district encompasses much of the park, he had, until only recently, been given veto-power over any Adirondack legislation. Thus one man, representing a relative handful of people, had control over the future of one-fifth of New York State, effectively blocking the ability of seventeen million others to be heard.

It is nearly six o'clock in the evening as I enter the village of Old Forge in the heart of the western Adirondacks. The village is another busy tourist center this time of year, although not as overbuilt as Lake Placid or Lake George. It takes only a few minutes to find my way to the public meeting on Governor Cuomo's proposed Adirondack legislation. I park my car and sign the list of those who wish to speak. I am early and the first to sign.

Perhaps there will only be a handful of people, I think hopefully. That would make it easier. But the crowd grows. By the time State Senator William Sears calls the meeting to order, over two hundred people fill the hall. I feel very alone and wish once again that I was somewhere on Long Lake fighting black flies.

The senator welcomes the audience and then proceeds to tell them that he is "unalterably opposed" to the governor's legislation. Having thus warmed up the crowd, he calls my name.

I stand and walk to the podium. Two microphones arch upwards and I lean into them as if for protection. I stare out over a sea of faces that are going to be very hostile once they hear my prepared remarks. I only want to get it over with. I make my points, speaking for about five minutes. When I finish, you could hear a pin drop in that auditorium. As I return to my seat, two people in the back of the crowd applaud. It is a less than fulfilling sound to hear two people out of two hundred applaud in a large hall. But I am grateful for it.

Senator Sears, to his credit, thanks me for taking the trouble to come and for my statement. During the next two and a half hours before I must leave to make the long drive home, not a single other speaker rises in favor of legislation to protect the park. People complain about having to paint their houses green so they will blend in on lakeshores or about having to set their homes back from the shorefront or about how they are tired of dealing with the Adirondack

Park Agency. There is as complete a case of universal denial as I have ever witnessed. "Development? What development?" is the prevailing attitude.

Driving home, alone in the dark, I feel many emotions. Relief that it is all over. Worry that no others had been willing to speak for the park. Fear that this great park will have no chance to survive if so many are only concerned with their livelihoods and the color of their houses.

But driving along mile after mile of empty black forest, I begin to hope that there may yet be time. There seems to be a lot of space here still, although I know this is partly an illusion caused by darkness. Darkness covers a multitude of sins, much the way people's everyday worries cover their ability to see larger issues.

Under the cloak of darkness, I never even see Sunday Rock as I leave the park. Could this be what the future holds? Will there no longer be any Sunday Rocks to let us know when we have left the busy world of man behind? Will there soon be nothing beyond Sunday Rock but more civilization?

Awakening

The sky has been overcast since dawn. A cold wind blows through the eel grass, and if I breathe deeply it hurts my lungs. I am breathing deeply because we are paddling hard, wanting to reach High Rock for a midday break.

High Rock is normally an easy morning's paddle on the first day of our week-long trip into the remote Five Ponds Wilderness Area of New York's Adirondack Park. The problem is that no matter how early a start we get, by the time we have packed the car, driven to Inlet, stored gear in the canoe, and are finally under way, it is invariably *late* morning.

Now the paddle has become tedious, but in a way that I don't mind. Already this trip has a special feel to it. We slip through the water in first one direction and then another.

The Oswegatchie River meanders like a rat in a maze, occasionally hesitating to loop around a waterlogged island of alders or to absorb an incoming stream. Like rats ourselves, we raise our heads from the toil to try to see our destination, but see instead only more loops and more alders. But like the rat, who sees only walls, we know something more waits at the end. We, like him, have done this before.

My shoulders have formed an aching ribbon of soreness that stretches from elbow to elbow and down my sides as well. I stare at the crimson sunburn on the back of Jim's head. His hair is jet black, and the red spot flashes beneath it like a blinking stoplight, forever signaling me, I like to think, to proceed at a measured pace.

Every year, that spot grows a bit larger. The burn is incongruous on this cold fall day that smells of flurries and the deep-freeze dead

The view from High Rock on the Oswegatchie River.

air I love to breathe in my grocer's meat locker. But Jim works outdoors, and the burn has been there since May.

I pause and waggle my shoulders, cheating, really, on our paddling rhythm. I try to avoid the little groans of stretching pleasure that will signal my failure to keep the pace, but Jim knows at once that I've decided to take a break, and without a word he shifts his own paddle and leans away forward to stretch his perennially stiff back.

We are nearly at High Rock anyway. The spruce and white pine have come down to meet the eel grass, and we drift lazily in toward shore. An enormous dead pine stump sticks out over the river. As we pass beneath it, I stare up in wonder.

"Stop!" I say loudly and drag my paddle. Jim looks back questioningly. With a growing sense of urgency, I grab hold of a branch and pull the canoe along the dead stump until I can reach the object of my attention.

Sticking out like a giant sea fan from the rotting wood is a fungus, its surface oddly mottled and smooth at the same time. I reach up, take hold, and break it free of the tree in one large piece.

Sitting back, I examine my prize with undiluted joy. Jim shakes his head and says, wisely, "That's going to get pretty heavy by the end of the week."

Jim is practical. But the fungus absorbs me, returning me twenty-eight years in time to the Adirondacks that I first knew.

As a boy of eleven, I am climbing Giant Mountain with a handful of other youngsters and our camp counselor. We are on a day trip from Camp Chateaugay. We are tired, exhausted, from the longest woodland hike of our young lives. But there, as we collapse on a mossy outcrop, is the fungus.

It is the same, almost, as the one I hold now in my hand. Twenty-eight years ago, that fungus was taken back to our camp in triumph. I can feel, even now, the toll in aching shoulders that it took to carry it so far. Yet I can remember arguing amongst ourselves for the privilege. Paraded before envious comrades, the fungus was painted a reddish ochre and inscribed with Indian (so we thought) symbols. It became the focal point of a camp-wide exhibit and show put on by our group.

I marvel at how vividly the memories return. I can even see the faces of best buddies long forgotten, since replaced by other best buddies through grade and high schools, through college and young working life, right down to Jim, sitting in front of me with his red spot, my present best buddy.

I spent only one month at that summer camp. My parents had toiled the labors of the pharaohs to convince me to go for even this short time. I had known I would hate it and had ended up loving it. Incredibly, when my month was over, the camp director called my parents and suggested that he would be glad to have me stay another month free of charge. Incredibly, I refused to stay, and I never went back. It is hard to fathom a young mind.

I had some earlier experience of the mountains so near my home town of Canton. My father and I had climbed Pitchoff Mountain. I remember the almost palpable fear I felt on those exposed reaches of steep rock near the summit. I can't remember now whether we made it to the top, but I remember the fear. Perhaps it was the opening salvo in a lifelong fear of heights that I still struggle with today when I have to work on the roof of my own home.

In such manner have the Adirondacks insinuated themselves upon me, invading my childhood fears and triumphs down to this moment as I sit staring at that fungus and thinking back over a quarter of a century.

Following the Chateaugay experience, I forgot about the woods. Oh, they were always there, lurking about the fringes of my life. I ventured into them occasionally to ski Big Tupper—never very well—out of the need to meet girls in high school. Now and again, there would be a trip to Catamount Lodge, St. Lawrence University's camp, to which we had access because my father taught at the college. A friend or two had camps we visited.

But I was busy, distracted by the political and cultural explosions of the sixties, the Adirondacks little more than a winter's impediment to the fastest possible route to Florida. The closest I would come to a wilderness experience was when I took a canoe out of the SLU boathouse, and then the purpose was to court a young lady, not isolate myself in the woods.

It was not until I was twenty-five that the mountains came back to me. I met Jim. Together, we began to discover that we had an equal joy in canoeing. Bit by bit, we dug further into the highlands, following the Grass, the Oswegatchie, and the Raquette back into their upper reaches.

One day, in a local store, I discovered Paul Jamieson's *Adirondack Canoe Waters—North Flow,* and I was hooked for life. My first edition of that classic of canoeing guides is now tattered and dog-eared and signed by the author. Paul was a colleague of my father's, and I knew him when I was a boy, but he had been just another adult. Now I saw him as a kindred soul, one who had the love of canoeing all those years ago.

Jim has stretched his back out. He picks up his paddle and dips it idly in the water. There is an insistence in his shoulders. He is hungry, and this *is* High Rock. I make room for my treasure in a canoe that has no more room for anything. I look up and follow Jim's gaze to the open summit of the rock where we will sit and eat as the Indians who once hunted this region must have done for hundreds of years.

I am thankful for that fungus, that I had the chance to reawaken my young feelings for the Adirondacks. I have since canoed in Labrador, sea kayaked in the cold North Atlantic, hiked mountains in the Swiss Alps, and snorkeled the warm waters off the island of Granada. But the Adirondacks will always be special, for they are so accessible. And they are home.

Day Trip

I sit on the sand, swatting occasionally at August deerflies. My companions and I are deep in the Adirondacks on the banks of one of its most popular rivers, the Raquette. The flies are of no account, for I am absorbing tales of these woods told by one whose memory stretches back four-fifths of a century. Clarence Petty, second generation Adirondack guide, former member of the Civilian Conservation Corps (CCC), forest ranger, member of Governor Rockefeller's 1968 Commission on the Future of the Adirondacks, and long-time chronicler of and advocate for wilderness preservation in these woods, is clearly in his element.

Yet even as I listen, I can not help thinking of another wilderness trip, one immortalized by the writer John McPhee. In *Encounters with the Archdruid*, McPhee recounts his journey through the Grand Canyon with conservation's guiding light of the past fifty years, David Brower. How similar, I think, must be the reservoirs of experience of men like David Brower and Clarence Petty. And how very rare they are.

Floating the Colorado with the nation's preeminent dam builder as Brower did on that trip was symbolic of the many encounters that men like David Brower and Clarence Petty have had to face. Brower hates all dams because they destroy rivers. During the many arguments that ebbed and flowed during that Colorado float, Brower said: "I'm prepared to say, here and now, that we should touch nothing more in the lower forty-eight. Whether it's an island, a river, a mountain wilderness—nothing more. What has been left alone until now should be left alone permanently."

13

Those words might sound extreme to some, but in fact, they were said a quarter of a century ago. A great deal of wilderness has been paved over since then.

Our day trip begins under clear skies at Corey's, the summer colony that had once been the center of operations for a handful of Adirondack guides, including Clarence Petty's father, at the turn of the century. From here, we pass through Stony Creek Ponds, down Stony Creek to the Raquette River, and on past Follensby Pond outlet to the boat launch on Route 3 outside Tupper Lake.

The excuse for this trip, as if one is needed, is to gather a handful of ardent Adirondack advocates together to explore the section of the river that connects with Follensby Pond. Privately owned and at risk of being broken up by developers, the fourteen-thousand-acre Follensby Park tract has become a symbol in the fight to preserve the Adirondack wilderness.

Our group is feeling somewhat relieved, almost giddy. Following three long, hard years battling to preserve endangered pieces of the park like Follensby, we had finally witnessed the passage of the Environmental Protection Act of 1993 by the New York State legislature.

It is an imperfect bill. Precariously financed and reliant on a real estate transfer tax that is in turn reliant on the questionable resurgence of the state's economy, the Act nevertheless will allow the governor to give a list of proposed land acquisitions to the legislature every year as part of the budget process. Properties like Follensby Pond, Whitney Park, and the Heurich estate on Lake Champlain (since acquired) will be given priority by the state.

However, compromise at this level of state government can lead to some very creative results. Originally, Governor Cuomo wanted a fund of $271 million a year, the Assembly had sought $248 million, and the Senate Republicans proposed $100 million. What we will have in the first year will be $25 million and not just for land acquisition but for landfill closure, recycling, waterfront revitalization, historic preservation and parks, and a host of other projects.

But the deal is done for now, and we are canoeing with Clarence Petty. Victories in the battle to preserve the Adirondacks have been few and far between in recent years. We are here for fun and for at least a brief celebration of the likely saving of Follensby Pond. (Since that writing, the owner of Follensby Pond has withdrawn his offer to sell to the state and the future of the tract is now very much in doubt.)

Clarence is describing his transformation from avid hunter to, as he grew older, one who has greater compassion for the animals of the forest. Having witnessed and guided countless hunting and fishing expeditions in the early days of the century, he is a receptacle of Adirondack lore—the best sort of receptacle, one who loves nothing more than to spin the narrative for the enrichment of his companions.

I close my eyes and see clearly the Adirondacks of the 1920s as Clarence regales us with stories of twenty-pound trout, of early loggers and catastrophic forest fires. He tells of a freshly killed deer many decades ago that raised its head long enough to look its killer in the eyes and shame him into giving up the hunt forever. Could that hunter have been Clarence, I wonder? And was that long-ago shot the one that spawned his own enlarged understanding of the wild?

Speculation. I later read an interview with Clarence in Charles Brumley's fine history, *Guides of the Adirondacks.* In it, Clarence names the hunter in question, one Carlos Whitney, a huge man who had shot many deer. "It just shows you how people change," Clarence said. "I see this happening in people as they get older. I think they have maybe a greater respect for life than the young people."

Later, on the river, I stay close to his canoe. I want to see how someone who has paddled for more than eighty years handles his craft. As I suspected, his skill is masterful. Once, when I was new both to paddling and to the Adirondacks, my partner and I were having lunch on the shore when a beautiful cedar canoe came round the bend. Its occupants were both silver-haired, but they paddled with such complete serenity and efficiency, and in such relaxed harmony with the river, that we watched them go by in a kind of trance. They seemed almost a part of the woods, as though we had inadvertently witnessed a moose and her calf swimming upriver, rather than two men paddling. My friend broke the silence after their passing to remark, "Someday, I hope we will look like that."

That is how Clarence looks in a canoe. He belongs there. Perhaps he was born in a canoe or maybe a guideboat—it was known to happen among the Indians and the voyageurs, and, I suspect, the early Adirondack guides.

Following our lunch break, Clarence glances upward and suggests that we might want to hurry along a bit. He pulls his blue raincoat out and puts it on. In response to someone's question, he smiles and says, "Gore-Tex. You wouldn't believe what this jacket cost.

Never would have purchased it myself. It was a gift, though, so I have to use it."

We launch our canoes and, sure enough, within twenty minutes the thunderstorm descends upon us with a vengeance. In an instant, the river is transformed. Sheets of rain pelt down driven by fierce gusts. Clarence is unfazed, paddling steadily, the rain dripping off the hood of his Gore-Tex parka.

We are not experiencing this storm alone. During the lunch stop, a group, including several very young girls, passes us. One of their canoes holds a novel collection of three paddlers, the middle of whom sits facing the stern, actually paddling against the others. The stern paddler is one of the youngest I have ever seen controlling a large craft. She can not be more than eight or ten. Still, she seems to know how to handle her paddle, even if her placement of the crew is somewhat suspect.

I reflect upon these young girls, perhaps starting out on their own Adirondack journeys of discovery. They have much to learn, and I envy them the years ahead. The Adirondacks they will experience may little resemble that described by our guide this day. But unknown to them, they have made a good start. They have shared a thunderstorm with an Adirondack original, Clarence Petty.

Busted on the Banks

On a warm spring day in 1986, we felt the call of the northern Adirondacks. There were three of us that sunny afternoon. David Trithart, an avid outdoorsman, and his brother, Bob, a paddling enthusiast and canoe builder from Vermont, joined me. We decided to do a short, round-trip canoe run on the South Branch of the Grass River from Newbridge to Copper Rock Falls. It was a pleasant, hour-long journey that would ultimately lead us to an unexpected investment of time, money, and energy.

At the end of our trip, as we pulled our craft from the river, we were confronted by a forest ranger and an officer from the Department of Environmental Conservation. After a short discussion with them, we were ticketed for trespassing. Our parked car had been spotted by the caretaker of the Twin Falls Hunting Club, whose duties included keeping a vigilant eye out for just this sort of transgression.

We would discover that it was not an unusual spot for canoeists to be ticketed. The Twin Falls club, which leases a large tract of land from Champion International, has long made it a policy to prosecute anyone coming onto their land, or what they consider to be their water, regardless of purpose. Ours had been the most innocuous of purposes—merely to *see* one of the most beautiful stretches of wilderness canoe waters in the state.

What *was* unusual about the situation, though, was our decision to fight the citations.

It was our contention that we had never been on the club's land, for we had launched our craft on a public road's right-of-way. The bridge crossing at this spot provides easy access to the wide and

Copper Rock Falls on the South Branch of the Grass River at very low water, about 1900.

deep channel of the South Branch. As for the river, although a land-owner who owns both sides of a moving stream may actually own the bottom of the river itself, under New York State law a passenger on a moving boat is *not* trespassing.

Our arraignment took place at the Town of Clare courthouse—a tiny room attached to the Clare Town Barn. The town justice turned out to be something of a surprise. A large man who sported a full beard and wore his hair pulled back in a ponytail, he greeted us dressed in bib overalls. He informed us that he had been the justice in Clare for eight years and was the lowest-paid justice in New York State.

We entered our plea of not guilty. The justice assured us that the DEC always sent an attorney to trials such as ours, but that if we agreed not to bring a lawyer, then he doubted one would be required from the DEC. In our ignorance, we consented. When our court appearance finally did take place, our request to tape-record the proceedings was denied. Thus, there would be no witnesses and no independent record of the trial, although David's wife, Rose, took copious notes.

In the weeks that followed our arraignment, we searched for maps and deeds in the St. Lawrence County Courthouse in Canton, spoke with the county superintendent of highways, and talked to Paul Jamieson, whose book, *Adirondack Canoe Waters—North Flow* had been our initial guide to the South Branch. We found a highway map that seemed to show a right-of-way at Newbridge that was more than twice the standard three-rod (or forty-nine-and-a-half-foot) easement granted.

At best, we felt we could win our case and perhaps establish a precedent for other canoeists. At worst, we believed the charges against us would be thrown out or dismissed. In short, our ignorance of the law was complete.

On the day of our trial we presented our evidence—a stack of information, documents, and maps. While I gave sworn testimony, the DEC officer's enormous police dog laid its head in my lap.

The DEC brought no maps, no deeds of ownership, no papers showing rights-of-way. The only evidence they had was a series of letters from the Champion and St. Regis paper companies stating that they believed the right-of-way to be fifty feet. While it was our contention that we had not exceeded even the allowed fifty feet, our map showing the extended right-of-way at Newbridge was not admitted into evidence.

There followed much talk of measurements and estimates of where we actually were when we took our canoes out of the water. The officers had made no measurements at the time of our citations but nevertheless came up with figures that neatly placed us just outside the fifty-foot right-of-way.

We had taken our own measurements, which we placed before the court. These were questioned by the DEC as not having been made by a certified tape measure. We began to see where things were going.

Although we would later discover that the letters from the paper companies were inadmissible as hearsay evidence, the justice found for the prosecution.

Perhaps the most telling statement of the entire proceeding came from the DEC officer who testified that the *prime function* of the DEC was to protect the rights of the private landowner.

We had never considered what the prime function of the DEC might be, but if we had, we might have said it was to protect the wilderness, to conserve the environment, or, perhaps, to promote reasonable recreation in the park.

Following the trial, we were informed in a cheerful manner by the justice that if we returned to the area again, we could expect to be ticketed again. There was always something the officers could find, we were told, a bald tire, improper parking, etc. Indeed, the justice said that parking anywhere on this road was illegal, as if the highway in question might be some sort of private carry for the hunting clubs in the area. What, we wondered, was some poor soul whose car broke down supposed to do? Clearly, the law of this land was here to protect the interests of the landlord and tenant, interests that did not include facilitating a canoeist's desire to paddle a lovely stretch of river.

It has been a hundred years since the public has been able to enjoy the special beauty of the South Branch of the Grass River. It is no small denial.

The South Branch ranges from quiet, flowing waters lined with forests of Eastern white pine, hemlock, and cedar, spruce-fir lowlands, and hardwoods to a spectacular series of cascades and waterfalls, the thunderous roars of which can be heard from half a mile away.

The river is remarkable not only for its beauty but for its variety of waters, ranging from flat water to Class V rapids suitable for experienced kayakers. From Newbridge to Degrasse, the drop is more than four hundred feet and requires numerous carries. But below this, from Degrasse State Forest to Russell, is a stretch of 11.5 miles that was acquired by New York State in 1979 as part of the Lampson Falls Tract. Here, despite the variety and difficulty of the canoeing conditions, even relatively inexperienced beginners can travel the route if prepared to line or carry their craft at times.

The river meanders in and out of the Blue Line below Degrasse, but is, nevertheless, accessible to the public. The trouble begins where you might least expect it—farther upstream, *within* the Adirondack Park boundaries on this river designated "scenic" under the Wild, Scenic and Recreational Rivers Act of 1975. Here, a 17.5 mile canoe route was recommended by the Adirondack Park Agency in its study report on the South Branch of the Grass, extending from the vicinity of the Route 3 bridge east of Cranberry Lake to the head of Rainbow Falls. But the land along this route is, as our case illustrates, privately owned, and the battle for easements has been long and difficult.

The state has now purchased a conservation and recreation easement to the upper reach of the South Branch. This access is closed to
the public during the big game hunting season. Access to the lower
section from the Route 3 bridge to Deerlick Rapids, a distance of 8.2
miles, was made possible in 1992 with a gift to the Nature Conser-
vancy of the roadbed of the Conifer to Cranberry Lake portion of the
old Grass River Railroad. The hunting clubs that lease the land still
consider the area their exclusive domain, however, and they patrol it
with great vigor, although changes in DEC policy in 1993 now give
them scant support for their complaints.

We appealed our convictions to St. Lawrence County Court,
where, after a year's wait, the court overturned the decision, stating
that there was a failure at the trial to prove beyond a reasonable
doubt that we were actually trespassing. But this decision did not
accomplish what we had desired—an implied easement at public
roads and bridges for purposes of gaining access to waterways.

And that was that—or so we thought. Although we gave some
consideration to performing the entire enterprise all over again, this
time prepared with camera and eyewitnesses to achieve the ideal case
evidence, we in fact did nothing more.

After three years, our case had receded to little more than a sad
memory of a spoiled spring afternoon. Then David had a conversation with Neil Woodworth, an attorney and Conservation Director for
the Adirondack Mountain Club. Woodworth was surprised to hear of
David's involvement in *People vs Angus*. He was no more surprised
than David, who listened in amazement as Woodworth proceeded to
fill him in on what had happened in our case.

It was through the efforts of Paul Jamieson, who has been waging
the battle to reopen lost canoe routes almost single-handedly for
many years, that Woodworth learned of our case. He latched onto it
as an example of the extent to which canoeing rights had been pur-
loined slowly but steadily over the past century by the paper companies and hunting clubs, and by other private landholders.

Because of his persistence, our case took on new importance. It
became a well-known and often-cited court test of navigability in
New York State. It was brought to the attention of the Governor's
Commission on the Adirondacks in the Twenty-first Century. In fact,
some of the commissioners actually visited the site of our infraction.

At this writing, it remains uncertain precisely where the state stands on matters of canoeing rights, easements, and rights-of-way. But restrictions caused by posting are changing. The DEC no longer prosecutes boaters passing through private land, and a bill to open all navigable waters within the Adirondack Park reappears in the legislature yearly, though so far unsuccessfully. Court tests are also underway and rulings to date have been favorable.

It would be nice to think that in some small way our spring afternoon on the waters of the South Branch may have helped to reopen a portion of the forbidden waters of the Adirondacks.

People and Places

A man is part of his canoe and therefore part of all it knows.

—SIGURD F. OLSON

An Excuse to Paddle

For a paddler, there are few places better to live than right here in the valley of the St. Lawrence River. Just to the south, literally in our backyard, lie the Adirondacks with their myriad lakes, rivers, and streams—the home and/or playground of "Adirondack" Murray, Noah John Rondeau, Frederic Remington, Theodore Roosevelt, and J. Henry Rushton, to name but a handful. It is a place where a canoe is as common a sight on top of a car as a surfboard is in Malibu.

Yet to surpass even this bounty, we need look no further than our northern neighbor, Canada. Her countless lakes and wild rivers make the Adirondacks seem almost a geological afterthought. That immense wilderness contains lakes virtually uncountable—more than five hundred thousand estimated in Quebec alone. It is the land of the great explorers and voyageurs who adapted the Indian canoe and occasionally even the Eskimo kayak to their own purposes.

Between these two vast wild lands lies the St. Lawrence River, often described as a highway to the interior of a continent, the river of a "thousand islands" where the rich and powerful once cavorted—and still do.

For a paddler, there could be no better place to live, and for a paddler who writes, there could be no more encompassing a subject. As I pen these words in late February, our rivers and lakes are frozen tight and unyielding. For many, the paddle has been put aside for the ice-fishing auger and the cross-country skis. But the true paddler can see beneath the ice. He can feel, even now, the breath of spring. Already, he secretly hefts the paddle, strokes those cedar strips, and pores over worn maps.

Planning a trip of a week or more can be a delight, one that absorbs winter evenings and turns February into April before you know it. But for many enthusiasts, it is the short, spur-of-the-moment jaunt that truly characterizes how they feel about this place of endless canoeing possibilities. There are those of you, I know, who remove your canoes from car racks only to place them in the next tantalizing little stream or pond or marsh.

And the Northlands are full of them. A day rarely passes when I don't drive across some tiny rivulet and wonder what lies just around that first bend. My favorite craft for this is my little Old Town solo, which weighs a scant thirty-three pounds and which fits nicely into the rear of my pickup. I can pull over and be on that stream in two shakes.

It's a bit like having a ticket to freedom with that little boat always at my beck and call. The contrast between cruising along a highway in air-conditioned comfort, perhaps listening to music or the news, and suddenly paddling up a silent and unknown stream is a transporting phenomenon like few others I have known. And the best part is, it's free.

I don't pretend to be an expert in all aspects of canoeing. Taken in its full measure, it is simply too broad a subject. Placid paddling, kayaking, racing, sea kayaking, wilderness, the environment, materials and equipment, historical figures, the opening of the inland Americas, the great explorers, the voyageurs, Native Americans . . . you get the idea.

But I have had a lifelong fascination with canoeing. The more I learn, the more I want to know, and sharing what I have discovered is the main goal of this book. I have canoed extensively in the Adirondacks over the last thirty or so years. I've also touched paddle to water in parts of Michigan, New England, Nova Scotia, Newfoundland, and Labrador and have sea kayaked the cold waters of the North Atlantic. But there are many more places I want to visit.

Writing gives me an excuse to do so.

A Trip into the Past

The canoe, also known as the dugout, kayak, bungo, or pirogue, has been discovered many times by man in many different lands. In North America, however, it has reached its most highly developed forms.

There were three basic types. In the Pacific Northwest, the hollowed-out log, or dugout, became the basis of a semiseafaring culture that plied the intricate archipelago. In the far North, the Eskimo stretched sealskin over a frame of driftwood or whalebone to make the kayak, which was paddled with a double-edged blade. And on the northern fringes of the American forest, the bark and later the birchbark canoe dominated a land of smaller trees, rapid rivers, and many carries that required lighter craft.

The natives of Canada never knew the wheel. Instead, the birchbark canoe was the craft of the Woodland peoples and, later, with various modifications, the pioneers and voyageurs. It became the means of early exploration throughout the interconnected lakes and rivers that made up the large part of the northeastern United States and Canada.

There is no better way to traverse these forested lands, and the Adirondack region is unsurpassed in its offering to the canoeist of chain lakes, rivers, and streams.

Variations on the theme of this sort of travel are endless. One can take the entire family, camping gear, and a small flotilla if so desired, using the many fine lean-tos sprinkled across the region. Or the individual can set out alone in a tiny solo canoe with little more than a tarp for protection against the elements. The trip may last a day, a week, or a month, can be leisurely, following routes long established

A sign of man's long presence in the Adirondacks—remnants of a crumbling dam.

with clearly marked carry trails, or can be as adventurous as one's imagination, bushwhacking one's own route using compass and topo map.

Many of the routes used are historic and are marked by signs of an earlier time—the aging docks and railpaths of the Marion River Carry Railroad or the few remaining signs of Everton, one of many abandoned lumbering settlements on the East Branch of the St. Regis River.

Despite the many hundreds of books written over the years purporting to be "definitive" guides to the correct methods and procedures of canoeing, the fact is that almost anyone can propel a canoe. I've seen experts in their nineties ride out a nasty set of rapids. I've also seen five-year-olds who were more than capable of moving their craft efficiently through the water. Those who want to engage in lengthy discourse on paddling technique and water classifications can certainly do so, but no one should be intimidated by the simple canoe.

Best of all, a trip into the wilderness is a trip into the past, to a place and a time before man put his indelible mark on the landscape. It can be exciting, renewing, good exercise, and a way to meet people. And it costs nothing. You can probably even borrow a canoe if need be.

In the words of Paul Jamieson, "Rivers are the museum galleries of the wilderness." And this is one museum where you don't need to worry about the parking.

The Osgood River

When I first saw the Osgood River, I was not impressed. Glimpsed a few times off the side of Route 30, it appeared small and too hemmed in by alders for my taste. But first impressions are deceiving.

As I paddled the little river that first time, my sense of completeness grew by leaps and bounds. Here was a river that met all of my requirements for an enjoyable paddle—a meandering stream and variable terrain, pristine surroundings, plentiful wildlife, and unexpected discoveries. I have yet to meet a more modest stream with more to offer. It remains one of my favorite trips anywhere.

The Osgood is the main feeder of Meacham Lake and is just fourteen miles long. It meanders through tamarack swamps and past steep piny eskers. There is a variety of vegetation, plenty of birdlife, and interesting geological features. But the crowning glory of this little stream is the series of ponds whose short outlets cut through the esker. I have rarely experienced a greater sense of discovery in the Adirondacks than when I have followed a tiny side flow into one of the lonely ponds. Completely surrounded by the steep-sided eskers, these quiet pools boast magnificent stands of white pine and bestow a feeling of isolation that gives one a sense of the primeval.

A few years ago, I was camping beside one of these ponds with my wife. Our site was high above the water and the view we had out over the surface of the misting lake was intoxicating. As we sat staring out at the last, lingering, blue light before nightfall, drinking in the utter silence, we were nearly scared out of our wits by the screech of an owl that swooped down over our heads.

The Osgood can be navigated all summer long, though I prefer autumn or early spring before bug season. My partner and I once started from the highest possible point of navigation. As soon as we were fully committed to the quickly moving current, the river narrowed until alders from each side blended together, forming a tunnel. The word "tunnel" is an embellishment, for that implies an opening. In fact, we spent an unpleasant thirty minutes blasting through alders, our faces scratched and clothing torn. I wouldn't try it again.

Yet I so love this little river that I always hesitate a moment before recommending it to friends. After all, there are only so many good places to pitch a tent, and though the trip can easily be made in half a day, I much prefer to take longer and immerse myself in the surroundings. But in fact, I have never met another soul, though this no doubt has much to do with when I choose to go there—early or late in the year and always midweek.

I am usually of two minds when informing others about my favorite spots—for obvious reasons. Telling a friend is one thing. Broadcasting a public notice through the media, another altogether. Still, I have known few paddlers who did not exhibit meticulous habits in the wild. Most have a reverence for such places and generally leave nothing behind them but ripples.

There will always be the exception, of course. But I firmly believe these exceptions are worth the cost to the alternative of closing the rivers completely. Rivers completely cut off from the eye of man, in perverse fashion, may suffer even greater depredations. In short order, they lose their admiring public. With the loss of awareness comes neglect. Large corporate owners and lumbering firms have been known to sell off such gems to developers at a moment's notice. Although the "forever wild" amendment has stood many challenges over the last century, vigilance will always be necessary, for little subject to the whim of man is truly forever—witness the present eagerness to drill for oil in Alaskan lands many had thought protected from such folly.

A few years ago, Earth First!, the radical environmental group, declared that the Five Ponds Wilderness Area south of Cranberry Lake should be completely off-limits to man. I could not disagree more strongly. I believe it is possible for people to visit these areas with minimal damage if—IF—they are not allowed to use motorized vehicles and if other backcountry rules, such as proper disposal of wastes, careful tending of fires, and so forth, are followed.

But if no one is allowed to see a beautiful place, how long can it be before there is no one left to care about it? Out of sight, out of mind. Then the only people who know about the spot are those who disobey the rules and go there on their dirt bikes and in their 4 × 4s. A pristine river that people can see develops fierce partisans who will fight to keep it that way. A river that no one can see only develops developers.

Literary Adirondacks

What do the following individuals have in common? Thomas Jefferson, Mark Twain, Albert Einstein, P. T. Barnum, Sylvia Plath, James Fenimore Cooper, Somerset Maugham, Al Jolson, Grover Cleveland, John Burroughs, Sophie Tucker, Joyce Carol Oates, Winslow Homer, Robert Louis Stevenson.

Give up?

Each one of these famous individuals spent time in, was often deeply influenced by, and perhaps even fell in love with the Adirondacks. In fact, the above list is of necessity a short one, a mere drop in the bucket. The natural beauty of the North Woods first burst upon the consciousness of the public in a major way with the publication of William H. H. Murray's book, *Adventures in the Wilderness*, in 1869. Poets, politicians, artists, showmen, scientists, athletes, and writers have been drawn to the Adirondack mountains ever since.

With good reason.

The Adirondacks present a paradox. Located just a few hours north of New York City (considerably longer in the era before automobiles), the region has long been one of the most accessible wildernesses in the entire nation. And yet the land was so remote that the highest headwaters of the Hudson were not discovered until more than fifty years after the discovery of the headwaters of the Columbia River in the Far West. And Mount Marcy, the highest peak in New York State, was not climbed until 1837, fully two centuries after the first ascent of Mount Washington in New Hampshire. Although other wilderness areas and parks within the United States have greater mountains, larger rivers, and grander lakes, the Adirondacks are

33

Adirondack camping trip, 1919. From left: Thomas Edison, Henry Ford, Harvey Firestone, Jr., John Burroughs, seated, with beard. Courtesy of the Adirondack Museum.

unique in that they bring all of these elements together in one vast park greater in size than Yellowstone, Grand Canyon, Glacier, Olympic, and Yosemite parks combined.

The rich and famous traveled to this wilderness for a variety of reasons. Some, like Mark Twain, were looking to escape the pressures of being world-famous celebrities. Others, like Robert Louis Stevenson, went out of necessity, to battle tuberculosis or other ailments considered treatable by the mountain air. After a single cold winter, Stevenson wrote: "The place is a kind of insane mixture of Scotland and a touch of Switzerland and a dash of America, and a thought of the British Channel in the skies." When spring finally came, he packed up and moved to Samoa for the remaining six years of his life.

Albert Einstein came to sail the mountain lakes, Winslow Homer to paint at the North Woods Club, John Burroughs for "wordless intercourse with rude Nature," Grover Cleveland to hunt for wolf, and

Sylvia Plath to visit her boyfriend in Saranac Lake during Christmas of 1952.

Not everyone had a completely positive experience. Einstein, who was unable to swim, capsized his sailboat repeatedly. Plath managed to break her leg while skiing, and Cleveland never did get his wolf.

But still they came.

There may be no other place that proved more popular among American presidents. In addition to Jefferson and Cleveland, Theodore Roosevelt, James Madison, Chester Arthur, Calvin Coolidge, and Benjamin Harrison all spent time in the North Woods. And no doubt others were once guests at the elaborate wilderness estates of the Rockefellers, Vanderbilts, Morgans, Whitneys, and Durants.

But first and foremost, it was beauty and solitude that brought the rich, the famous, and the powerful to the Adirondacks. And though the mountains are not the same virgin wilderness that once enthralled Emerson at the Philosophers' Camp of 1858, they can still offer inspiration aplenty to those willing to look for it.

Metro Canoe

They say you have to find your good times where you can. A friend who lives in New York City was recently telling me about some locals who had canoed down the Hudson and all the way around the island of Manhattan. He was very excited about this and regaled me at length on the wonders of canoeing the great metropolis.

Now, canoeing the East River, in my book, ranks right up there with punting in the Persian Gulf.

Just think of it! The smell of Third Avenue after the garbage strike, the magnificent vistas through the late afternoon smog, the colorful flocks of seagulls coasting in to feed at Fresh Kills landfill, the Donald's helicopter roaring overhead, the distant drum of gunfire . . .

Ah, wilderness!

New Yorkers may think I'm being cynical about their homeland. But I've always felt a certain amount of pity for paddlers in the Big Apple. Compared with the almost inexhaustible resources of our own Adirondacks and St. Lawrence River Valley, what could the big city possibly have to offer?

As it turns out, quite a lot.

For the past several years, the Department of Parks and Recreation has had a system of official launch sites for canoes and kayaks. This system, the first of its kind in a major city in the United States, spans every borough of New York.

The variety of offerings is really quite impressive for a major metropolitan area, and although you won't find the sort of pristine surroundings that we have come to expect in the Adirondacks, the selection is nonetheless intriguing.

Within easy paddling distance one can find five-hundred-foot natural cliffs, excellent bird-watching in vast marshes, a graveyard of old tugs and barges, monolithic skyscrapers, and ships of every nationality and type. Paddling about the aging piers and peering in on a city bustling with activity can give one a fascinating new perspective on New York.

The city has wisely exploited this idea in a time of budget problems, for the cost has been negligible. Canoes and kayaks need no elaborate breakwaters or ramps or any other special construction and upkeep. Enthusiasts can transport their craft on top of cars or even take the subway to one of the sites if their boat is of the folding variety. Such collapsible craft have been designed to fit neatly into easily carried hand luggage. They rest unobtrusively on the floor beside you as the subway delivers you to your destination. Assembly can be completed in just a few minutes on site. Don't forget your mace.

I've spent enough time in New York City to know it is not where I would choose to go canoeing. But if I had to live there, I can think of few more pleasurable ways to get away from it all. The noise and clatter of the city seem to disappear out on the water. I confess I have never canoed the East River and environs. But I have ridden the Staten Island Ferry and the views of the city from such a vantage point are breathtaking.

The Metropolitan Canoe and Kayak Club offers a free guide to the launch sites. It includes information on transportation, nearby eateries and restrooms, references on tides and currents, degrees of difficulty, and suggested itineraries. Information on permits and the guide can be had from any Parks Department office.

Well, my big-city friend is still at it, and he swears that on a good day, the fragrance coming off Fresh Kills is rather like that of seaweed. He wants me to come down and experience all of this beauty with him.

I told him I just couldn't make it. But I'm quite satisfied with this fine fellow. After all, he doesn't bother to come up to the mountains and make them even more crowded than they already are. He's too busy kayaking the canyons of the East River.

I couldn't be happier for him.

Solo

I'm just back from an outing on the Little River near Canton. Having grown up in this small northern New York village and having attended St. Lawrence University there, I think I can honestly estimate that this was somewhere around my two hundredth trip on this particular little stream. I have canoed her in the fifties, sixties, seventies, eighties, and nineties. Five decades. If I live long enough, perhaps I will make the century circuit and paddle her in the year 2050. A very long shot.

For some, it may become tedious to repeat the same trip so many times. This is hardly wilderness after all. But familiarity breeds its own rewards. I was struck on this day, as I am almost every time I paddle this river, by how rarely I meet anyone. Certainly less than 10 percent of my trips have involved an encounter with other paddlers. This is really quite extraordinary when you consider that it is a small gem of a river, is on the outskirts of a village of some five thousand people, and skirts a university with two thousand students.

Where is everybody?

The Little River has a rich history of canoeing. There have been a number of canoe liveries, some quite extensive, with docks and large buildings dating back to Rushton's time. Some wonderful pictures of these early facilities can be seen at the St. Lawrence County Historical Association in Canton. Ladies in full Victorian finery sport along the river under their parasols, much as their counterparts strolled St. James Park in London or the Champs Élysées in Paris.

Today, the river is much more quiet. I had thought that paddling was enjoying something of a renaissance. There are more boat shows, canoe races, magazines about canoeing, boat weekends, canoe clubs, and so forth. And yet, here I am out on one of my favorite day trips and there is not a soul around.

I should admit that I am out on a workday (though that never stopped any student I ever knew) and that it is still March. The day is cool, about thirty degrees, but sunny, and the river should be inviting enough to anyone really serious about stealing their outdoor moments. In fact, canoeing in the St. Lawrence Valley this time of year is not all that unusual. I have paddled up the Little River in every month of the year—yes, that includes January.

But I am alone. And, as Garbo said, it's what "I vant to be." The trouble is, it bothers me. Can I really be the only one among the seven or eight thousand people within a mile of this easily accessible river who wants to be out here on a beautiful sunny afternoon?

From an environmental standpoint, it worries me that there is so little interest in such a valuable resource. If no one cares, how long can it be before some developer lines these meandering shores with condominiums? Most of the land belongs to SLU now, but who is to say what budget pressures of the future could bring?

Today, I see a number of blue jays and gray squirrels, a hawk, possibly an osprey, though I am too far away to be sure, and a white-tail. She is a doe, and I don't spot her until after she hears me. She takes a couple of leaps, then stops still, uncertain where I am. I float in toward shore until I am less than a dozen feet from her and watch as she turns her head from side to side trying to pinpoint my location. She apparently doesn't expect me to be on the water. Finally, she looks straight into my eyes. In an instant, she bounds into the woods, white tail bobbing, and is gone.

On another trip on this stream, I saw one of only three pileated woodpeckers that I've ever seen. Close to the size of a small chicken, these impressive birds never fail to amaze. This one was joyfully hammering away at a dead elm, huge chips of wood flying in all directions.

Today, there is a great deal of ice damage to the trees from the recent ice storm. Small limbs dangle everywhere and entire trees have split along weak forks. The newly exposed wood stands out, a glaring bone-white against the prevailing spring shades of brown and gray.

Farther along, I pass under the footbridge built by SLU students (there must be a few who care after all) and decide to cozy into a small sidestream that still has a thin film of ice on it. My canoe rides through the barrier like a diminutive icebreaker plowing up the Hudson straits. The experience reminds me of another encounter on this stream. Paddling serenely along, I rounded a bend and suddenly thought I had been transported to Lilliput. Baring down on me were a pair of gray navy battleships. Perhaps the most unexpected encounter I have ever had on the water, these two completely realistic ships were each about six feet long, sported full turrets, and operated guns that were firing BBs. The minute warships were run by remote control by a man who had built them himself and who was just up the shore.

Nearly at the rise where students have built a lean-to beside the cross-country ski trail, I am out of time and turn to begin the downstream journey. Just a few meanders from the car, I once again hear the loud hammering of the woodpecker. Could it be another pileated? I stop paddling and drift towards the sound. It is a very loud banging and I think it can only come from the pileated, but I cannot locate him. I strain, looking all about, and then I see him. It is only a small hairy woodpecker. He has been working on a stump not half-a-dozen feet away right on the riverbank. He was so close that I was looking right over him into the trees in the distance.

A small disappointment on an afternoon of large pleasures. And once again, I have had the river to myself. Where is everyone?

Leaving Rushton in Peace

It's a good thing J. Henry Rushton isn't alive today. The world-famous builder of finely crafted cedar lapstrake canoes and guideboats would likely turn over in his grave if he knew about some of the goings-on in the world of canoeing in the late 20th century.

Although he made some popular decked canoes, to my knowledge Rushton never made any kayaks, but it certainly might have given him pause if he had witnessed Randy Fine set the new world record for Eskimo rolls in Biscayne Bay, Florida. Fine set his dervishlike standard in two hours by completing 1,796 revolutions. Rushton understood the human need for competition and was one of the founders of the American Canoe Association, an early racing sponsor. But one can only imagine him scratching his head in complete dumbfoundedness if he had come across Fine practicing his skill on the waters of the Grass River.

Fine stated that he just liked setting standards that other people might never even consider challenging. Following his record-setting stint, Fine's hands were covered in blisters, his ankles rubbed raw, and his legs so cramped that he could only walk backwards for an hour afterwards. A loner, you say? Something of a fruitcake? Well, consider that Fine does not even hold the record for the fastest thousand Eskimo rolls. No, Ray Hudspith has that record, which he achieved in just 34 minutes, 43 seconds. Go ahead, do the math. That's roughly thirty rolls a minute—one every two seconds. I can't even roll over in bed that fast.

Or consider Rushton's amazement to find water enthusiasts eschewing his finely made and once immensely popular craft in favor

A Rushton-style canoe of the "Sairy Gamp" type, at an antique dealer's display at the Adirondack Museum. Rushton's canoes are still highly collectible and are often copied by builders.

of the body board. Using four-and-a-half-foot-long chunks of crafted ethafoam, the body boarder prepares for work by suiting up in crash helmet, wetsuit, kneepads, and swim fins. He then throws himself into waters that reach Class IV whitewater ratings. A few years ago, before the body-boarding craze really took off, there was a fellow who "swam" down Mt. Everest using a similar getup but with a single float bag in place of the board. He threw himself into the highest stream of glacial meltwater he could find and rode the turbulence all the way to the bottom. Someone even made a film of the feat. Could you blame them? How else would anyone ever believe the story?

Rushton's boats were shipped to France, Egypt, the Philippines, and Australia. They were used throughout the Adirondacks by the famous writer George Washington Sears, also known as Nessmuk, and on rugged expeditions to the headwaters of the Mississippi. But there is one record Rushton would have a hard time believing. Call it the lifetime achievement in canoeing award. Fritz Lindner of Berlin, Germany, paddled an incredible 64,278 miles by canoe from 1928 to 1987. I'd still like to know how the *Guinness Book* verified that one.

The Rushton boat shop produced a wide variety of guideboats, rowboats, skiffs, and canoes. But today's specialization would have amazed the diminutive businessman. Take the Tsunami X-l Rocket kayak, for example. This boat was made for sea touring and surfing. Made out of kevlar, it boasts three watertight compartments, dolphin bow, kickup rudder, and grooveline. It is sixteen feet long and just twenty-one inches wide.

Some of Rushton's boats didn't even have seats. The paddler sat or kneeled on the bottom. It is hard to imagine, therefore, what he would have made of today's new saddle systems for open canoes. The saddle looks remarkably like it sounds. It was designed to give paddlers a lower center of gravity to improve stability, balance, and control. And by removing the low thwarts of traditional canoe seats, the danger of snagging one's feet during turnover was eliminated. These saddle systems are made from rotomolded plastic or solid foam. The cost? As much as $300 or roughly the original purchase price of ten early Rushtons.

J. Henry would probably be glad he's not around to see these derivative fashions, the plastics, foams, and gels, the fiberglass, ABS, and kevlars. He might not have even guessed that some of these contraptions were boats. His understanding of the function of the Tsunami X-l Rocket may have been little better than if he had been looking at a hydrofoil.

But more than ninety years after his death, boat enthusiasts still admire and covet Rushton's beautiful creations. It would seem unlikely that such will ever be the fate of the Tsunami Rocket.

Adventure (rerun)

Once, in a spirit of high adventure, my friend Jim and I spent several weeks traveling in Newfoundland and Labrador. Our goal was to canoe some truly wild rivers—a goal only partially realized as we managed to choose a summer of uncommon drought. Still, the adventure was realized in my mind, if nowhere else, and I find myself thinking of it often.

Adventure! The word calls forth images of Ernest Shackleton and Sir Edmund Hillary, the search for the Northwest Passage, Vikings braving the cold North Atlantic, and even the heroes of my childhood fantasies, Davy Crockett, Tarzan, and Mowgli. These images, fictional and real, have all tumbled together to give the word "adventure" a vivid and genuine meaning. Whatever else, adventure was always serious business.

But the world has changed, and so has the word.

Today, travel to the highest mountain in Tibet and you will find an expedition of scores of cameramen, transport crews, and media people all in support of a single man who wants to ski down Everest, or another who dons aqualung and wetsuit in order to "swim" down the great mountain's frigid glacial streams.

Journey to the Bering Strait, and you might see a middle-aged woman swimming from America to Russia in waters so cold she must dodge icebergs.

On the frozen Arctic Ocean, a man is attempting to be the first to ride a motorcycle to the North Pole. In the South China Sea, another has just completed a grueling open ocean voyage windsurfing on a fiberglass board. And a blind man recently undertook the first "blind" crossing of the Atlantic. In what must be one of the great understatements of any age, he said: "It's not going to be easy."

Or consider the re-creation of adventurous exploits in the name of commerce. Stephen Spielberg reproduces Shanghai of the 1920s complete to thousands of extras dressed in costumes of the era. On a frozen wasteland, a public television company reconstitutes the tortures of the ill-fated Shackleton crew. And in nearly every country, wars past and present are perpetually recast and refilmed to supply TV networks with late-night adventure reruns.

In the face of such incredible and often outrageously expensive feats, what can be left for the ordinary set of adventurers?

What, I wonder, does a starving African family think when they see a Land Rover, patriotic flags flying, roar past their outstretched rice bowls, as it competes in a trans-African safari? How do boatloads of starving Haitian or Vietnamese refugees comprehend that windsurfer who glides past them on his high-tech board dressed in a rubberized wetsuit?

The gap between what adventure was and what it has become is as great as the distance that separates that starving refugee from a Leona Helmsley in her penthouse. Today, adventure appears to represent more an act of self-discovery than one of physical exploration—of psychological absorption rather than societal obligation.

There is something in us, it seems, that will always need adventure, so that as the real ones become used up, we stand ever-ready to create new ones, however absurd and remote from real life. What is the point, after all, in attempting to "re-create" Amundsen's march to the South Pole, if one uses modern down clothing, high-protein-density dehydrated foods, and satellite positioning devices to determine longitude and latitude?

Adventure is escapism in today's world. It enables us to forget, however briefly, the bewildering and fast-moving changes that are overwhelming our crowded planet. It can, quite simply, make us feel relevant again.

And so, in the absence of new frontiers, we create false ones based on doing a thing faster or without oxygen or by a more dangerous route or simply in a manner so ridiculous that no one ever thought of it before—motorcycling to the North Pole.

What makes us "feel" relevant has at last become truly irrelevant. We go four-wheeling past the gaunt faces of the starving.

The King's Trees

There is a place on the Chubb River, deep in the Adirondacks, where the stream takes a wide turn and heads into a large, open marsh. Here, a tall row of sturdy, windswept white pines clings to the last bit of high land. The trees tower above the surrounding country—some of the best remaining wilderness in the lower forty-eight states.

The Chubb is a magical river—slow-moving, tannin-colored and enticing in its many varieties of landscape. Incredibly, we are barely two miles from the heart of Lake Placid, but the solitude is complete. The meandering river works its way into the forest preserve of the High Peaks Wilderness Area where we are treated to vistas of mountains on every side. Nye Mountain, at 3895 feet, and Street Mountain, at 4166 feet, fill the horizon and come back into view again and again as the curves of the stream snake us back and forth.

But as impressive as the broad flank of Nye Mountain is, it is that stand of white pine that comes back to haunt my thoughts long after the trip is over. For the white pine is without doubt the most magnificent of the eighty or so species of trees that grow in New York State.

Before the early pioneers went to work on the valuable tree, virgin specimens reached two hundred and fifty feet in height and as much as five feet in diameter. Some were nearly four hundred years old. The great forests of the 17th century were a mix of hemlock, giant red spruce, and white pine, with large stretches of thick-barked oaks that were helped along by the Indians' frequent burning of the landscape to attract game. It was not until after the primeval pines and spruce were cut down, however, that the hardwoods moved in, in truly impressive numbers.

*A large white pine threatens to impede paddlers on the Oswegatchie
River.*

According to Maitland DeSormo in *The Heydays of the Adirondacks*,
the plateau along the western shore of Lake Champlain stretching
back to the Adirondack foothills was originally covered with "a massive growth of snagbark or first-growth white pines, the big whites,
the monarchs of the forest."

But the early settlers went to work on these trees quickly. The
long, straight, nearly knot-free timbers made for prime building material. They were used to construct everything from homes, barns, and
churches to ships, wagons, and roads. The trees were cut and hewed
into square timbers, which were then lashed together and floated
downriver via, for example, the Richelieu River (outlet of Lake Champlain) to the St. Lawrence, where they were sold at market in Quebec.
Often, the early loggers sold the magnificent trees at or below cost.
Again, according to DeSormo, "Old-timers reported that after their
rafts had been sold and their expenses paid, they had enough to get
home provided they didn't drink or smoke and could walk fast."

But perhaps nothing had a more profound impact on the white pine than its value to shipbuilders for the construction of masts. The British and French navies both used the tree extensively to the point that a prime mast specimen could bring as much as three or four thousand dollars. Indeed, many of the British and French ships that fought one another at Trafalgar in 1805 were equipped with masts and spars and even planking from the Adirondack woods.

So valuable did the trees become to the British navy that they came to be called the "King's Trees." As early as 1691, a clause was inserted in a new Massachusetts Bay Colony charter reserving to the Admiralty all white pines "of the diameter of twenty-four inches and upwards at twelve inches from the ground." The King's men marked examples of these royal trees by giving them three whacks with a hatchet. This came to be called the mark of the Broad Arrow.

Even so, the pioneers were not terribly concerned with the King's needs, and poaching of the big trees continued. Finally, in 1722, the Crown extended the Broad Arrow protection to all white pines in the colonies regardless of size. But the slaughter of the whites continued, and by the mid-1800s, loggers were already moving westward, for most of the big trees on the East coast had been cut. Indeed, at various times during the 18th and 19th centuries, farmers and loggers managed to harvest all but about 2 percent of the Northeast's vast forests.

But the white pine is a survivor. It begins bearing seeds at a young age and grows quickly, outpacing other species when faced with sunny open areas. Thus, abandoned farmland and old burn sites become prime growth spots for the resurgent trees.

In the summer of 1995, many of the virgin pines that lined the shores of the Oswegatchie River deep in the Five Ponds Wilderness Area were destroyed by a sudden, violent windstorm. It was a devastating loss to the Adirondack preserve and to recreationists familiar with the area. Yet despite such occasional acts of God, it is today estimated that as much as 10 percent of the Adirondacks may consist of white pine.

It is comforting to know, as one floats past those mighty sentinels along the Chubb, that this forest species that has so much history will surely survive. For in the words of Henry David Thoreau, a noted lover of trees, "Nothing stands up more free from blame in this world than a pinetree."

Testosterone Poisoning

I've been thinking about risk. I've never been a big fan of excessive risk. Although I have been in a few tight situations, they were almost never by choice. I went sea kayaking once on the cusp of a hurricane, unbeknownst to either me or my partner. The wind and waves we experienced were the most intense I've ever been in, and we were probably lucky not to get into serious trouble.

But some people seek risk, and by definition trouble, when they go into the out-of-doors. Mountain climbers, Olympic downhill skiers, Arctic expeditioners, and the like enjoy explaining to the incredulous faces about them that they simply cannot feel truly alive unless they are in danger of losing their lives. Take Joe Kane, for example, a white-water kayaker who has tumbled down remote and wild streams like Peru's Colca River. "Risk," Kane says in a *National Geographic* article, "is the price you pay to reach a place that can blast your spirit clean." That Kane and others can say this stuff with a straight face is, I suppose, a kind of talent in itself. My response to them is: "Once you're dead, you'll never feel as alive as I do."

But still they insist that it's all a matter of "calculated" risk. You understand the degree of danger and you make the proper preparations and from then on it's up to the fates and your own skill.

I have no doubt that what they are doing is exciting. And I would not for a moment question the feelings of fulfillment that come with being in the out-of-doors. Young men and women should be seekers of adventure. I've experienced such feelings often. But if they want to talk about risk with me, I will ask them, what about the risk of losing everything by dying at the age of twenty-five or thirty? Do they really want to feel "alive" so much that they are willing to give up the things that actually make up living—things like having children and watching them grow, success in work, travel, good food, and on and on? Is that moment of feeling "alive" worth the next sixty years of actual living?

I think not. In fact, I think that if they took the time to really consider what is at stake, they might agree. How many Everest expeditions have I watched on TV where the group sets out brimming with good cheer and ends up after the death of one or more of their members full of shock and despair. What, one wonders, did they expect to feel? Taking undue risk in order to feel fulfilled shows, I believe, nothing more than an incredible lack of imagination. The world is a fascinating place, with more things to amaze and amuse than we can ever grow tired of. I would no more consider giving up sixty years of that exploration of life in exchange for a moment's adrenaline than I would consider committing suicide while I was still in perfect health. You can have your bungee jumping, thank you very much.

Perhaps the whole business is really about testosterone and peer pressure and the drive to be macho. Men have a lot of trouble coming to grips with these sorts of things. Another reason we do it, of course, is to impress women. But most women I know tend to feel the same way I do about this stuff.

So if your goal is to impress the girl next door, think again. Once past the age of six or seven, most females tend not to react in the desired manner.

Editing for Humanity

I picked up a book called *The Thousand Mile Summer* recently. Written by Colin Fletcher and published in 1964, it's about the author's hike from Mexico to Canada by way of the California desert and the High Sierra.

I've enjoyed some of Fletcher's other work, especially the wonderful tale of his walk through the Grand Canyon called *The Man Who Walked Through Time*. He has an engaging style and misses little of interest as he crosses the terrain. So I was looking forward to reading this earlier work when I came across a passage that made me look at the writer in an entirely new light.

While hiking through Death Valley, Fletcher rounds a bend and comes face to face with a rattlesnake. Instead of the enlightening description of this creature of the desert that I expected, he writes: "Across the trail, five feet ahead, stretched a sinuous brown evilness." The author proceeds to stalk the snake, which poses no threat whatsoever to himself, and eventually to destroy it by smashing it with a stick. The creature takes considerable time to dispatch completely. All the while, Fletcher describes the "waves of evil" he feels emanating from it.

My amazement at this display coming from a man whom I had considered one of the most thoughtful and considerate chroniclers of nature can scarcely be described. I tried to rationalize his actions. He must have been surprised and scared by the snake in some manner and reacted quickly. But in fact, he displays not the slightest regret for his actions. Indeed, only a few pages further on, he describes killing two more rattlers in the space of twenty minutes. Again, he dwells on the "evilness" of the reptile.

Fletcher's attitude would be very unlikely to appear in any naturalist's book today. It is difficult to believe that things could have changed so thoroughly in the past thirty years, but such would seem to be the case. Although a sensitive observer of nature for many years, the author has no hesitation whatsoever in dispatching rattlesnakes simply because they are rattlesnakes.

It reminded me of the way in which early Americans (and some later ones too) methodically went about the work of destroying other predators: the mountain lions, wolves, and even hawks and eagles. Any creature that didn't serve man's own interests was simply in the way and worthy of dispatch.

Still, I continue to believe we have learned a lot since 1964. We have learned that the balance of nature is terribly subject to man's various foibles, fantasies, and fears. We have learned, for example, that wetlands, once thought of as places of evil just as Fletcher thought of that snake as evil, are in fact among the most important crucibles of life.

We are making progress, albeit at an excruciatingly ponderous pace. As a species, we don't much like to admit our faults. The result is that it sometimes takes the passage of generations for real change to occur. It didn't take Colin Fletcher that long, I am happy to report. Later on in his desert hike, after talking with a ranger, he changes his thinking about snakes and leaves them in peace.

That's progress.

I'm relieved that Fletcher doesn't feel the same way today about rattlesnakes that he did thirty years ago. His beatings of snakes would never make it past the first junior editor who read his material today. "Too many animal lovers out there," the editor would jot in the margin. "Better leave this out."

The River of Nuts

Browsing through Nathaniel Bartlett Sylvester's 1877 book, *Historical Sketches of Northern New York and the Adirondack Wilderness*, one comes across an interesting discussion about the names of various Adirondack rivers.

Most rivers go through name adaptations and variations over the years. The Grass(e) River debate has continued for at least a century and a half. The river still has the (e) attached in most newspapers, road signs, etc., even though it was apparently an affectation by some who felt it gave more style to the word.

Paul Jamieson, who has written about the debate, argues convincingly that the river got its name from the grass meadows at its mouth. He writes: "Antiquity is on the side of 'Grass' . . . the 1798 Patent of the Macomb Purchase . . . supports the view that the river we all love was named, more than 180 years ago, not by an unbalanced Frenchman with panache, but by a plain Anglo-Saxon who saw meadows, believed the evidence of his senses, and had the foresight to recognize a promising resource, our grass." I have accepted Jamieson's argument and have dropped that *e* from my own usage. Those who remain doubtful might consider reverting to the Indian name, Ni-Kent-Si-A-Ke, which means "the place where many fishes live."

Here are a few other early names as described by Sylvester. It would be wise to remember that precise authentication of Indian names is often impossible and that there are several feasible alternatives for virtually every example cited herein.

Ra(c)quette River—from a French word meaning snowshoe. The name was suggested by the shape of a wild meadow at its mouth and was first applied to the river by a Frenchman named Parisein during the early French occupancy. The Indian name was Ta-Na-Wa-Deh or "swift water."

Indian River—O-Je-Quack or "the river of nuts."

Oswegatchie River—O-Swa-Gatch or "the river that runs around the hills," referring to the large bends or oxbows it forms on its course.

St. Regis River—Ah-Qua-Sus-Ne or "the place where the partridge drums," alluding not to the bird at all, but rather to the rumbling sound made by surface pressure on the ice on some parts of the stream during the winter.

Salmon River—Gan-Je-Ah-Go-Na-Ne or "sturgeon river."

Chateaugay River—named after a chateau called the gay chateau, or Chateau-Gai that stood on the bank of the St. Lawrence, at its mouth.

Moose River—Te-Ka-Hun-Di-An-Do or "clearing an opening."

Beaver River—Ne-Ha-Sa-Ne or "crossing on a log."

Given that Northern New York was often hotly disputed territory, claimed at various times by the Algonquins of Canada, the Iroquois of Central New York, the French colonists of the St. Lawrence and the Dutch and English settlers of the Hudson, it is not surprising that there were many different names and variations over the years.

Rather than spend too much time arguing over which names are the more correct, we might as well enjoy the historical diversity. After all, the Adirondacks are home to twenty Long Ponds, ten East Ponds, sixteen Clear Ponds, twenty Mud Ponds, ten Round Ponds, ten Duck Ponds, and twelve Otter Ponds. So, I'll take an Oswegatchie, a Gay Chateau, or a River of Nuts any day.

Long Lake Revisited

A shiver of anticipation comes over me as we enter Long Lake. How many times have I been in this spot? I can no longer remember. This cold fall day began with flurries and a glowering sky that has since fulfilled its promise. Now, in early afternoon, the clouds hang gray and low and full. The wind is punishing, not gale force, but certainly gusting hungrily in that direction.

Just holding our sixteen-foot Mad River canoe steady takes concentration. We stare down the seemingly endless expanse. I am exhausted just thinking about the toil ahead. Whitecaps and a three-foot chop rock us unmercifully, the cold water spraying us with a frigid mist.

We have done this before, of course, on countless lakes. But why must the wind *always* blow against paddlers in a hurry? Surely this is a research subject worthy of some aspiring young meteorologist.

Normally, we would land and wait for the storm to die, perhaps running the full length in the quiet of evening. For Long Lake can be as different in wind and calm as two lovers. Once, on a still evening under moonlight, its mirrored surface held our canoe as though floating in space and our passage was nearly as silent. But, alas, we are on a schedule—only so many days, so many nights until duty, family, work reel us back in.

Still, I am exhilarated. This sort of effort, at heart, is what a wilderness trip is all about. Sometimes it is hard to think of Long Lake with its cabins and year-round homes, its bridge and hamlet, and even its seaplane port as wilderness. But I know in my heart, staring into that maelstrom of froth and wind, that wilderness it is. This wind is just as wild, this water just as cold, our canoe just as flimsy, and our paddling expertise just as crucial as they would be if we were in Hudson Bay.

Water means a lot to me. Many of my happiest times have come when I could put as much of it as possible all around me. Even so, our relationship had a rocky beginning. I first crossed the Atlantic when I was twelve. My primary memory of that journey is one of being flat on the floor under the sink in our tiny stateroom. Seasick. I spent two full days under that sink, so miserable that I refused to be moved. One of the earliest childhood images that I can still call up in remarkable detail is the peculiar twisting of the piping of that sink.

Since then, I've punted on the Thames, steamered up the fiords of Norway, gondolaed on the Grand Canal, cruised past the castles of the Rhine, and ferried down the Bosporus. I've swum in the Mediterranean, Black, Aegean, Adriatic, North, and Baltic seas as well as the Pacific, Atlantic, and Caribbean.

You see, I know my water.

For all this, I have no hesitation when asked my favorite body of water. It is that section of the Raquette River from the end of Long Lake to Axton. And in a larger sense, it includes the chain of lakes and connecting carries that stretch from Blue Mountain Lake through Raquette and Forked Lakes into Long Lake and on down to Tupper.

We go back a long way, this water chain and I. It has a rich history of Indians and fur traders, pioneers and wealthy capitalists, sportsmen and entrepreneurs, writers and artists. And I have my own personal history encompassing the many trips I've had, the close calls, the wet nights, the aching shoulders, the many campfires and good companions.

As a result, when I travel these ancient routes, each trip becomes a kind of inner journey, a flooding of memories of good and bad, but never indifferent, times. That campsite on Utowana Lake is where I took those two vividly contrasting pictures of Jim standing in the same spot looking out first at a lake wild with whitecaps and then, barely an hour later, still as glass. This lean-to is where I spent one of my first nights in the mountains, shivering for hours in my sleeping bag, certain that every sound was from a hunger-crazed bear snuffling about in my gear.

Here at the head of Long Lake—where we now contemplate today's challenge—is the campsite we once found after two long, rainy days on the chain. We had piled on the miles that second day, to avoid having to make another wet camp. It was late in the afternoon, we were soaked, and a heavy fog was making the gloom that much worse. Suddenly, across the water came the last sound we expected, the strains of a violin. We stopped paddling and floated, not believing our own ears.

Then the music stopped, and as we floated closer to shore, we heard voices speaking German. In hesitating English, someone called out: "Please—where are we?"

We pulled ashore and struck up a halting conversation with two eighteen-year-old German youths who had flown straight over to the Adirondacks for a three-week trip on this marvelous wilderness river system they had heard about. They had little gear and no maps and had been out already over a week. They were completely and utterly lost—as lost as one can be, at any rate, on upper Long Lake. They were scarcely a hundred yards from a major highway, so their situation was hardly dire. But I have never before or since come across two less-prepared individuals in the wild.

We spent the night with them, a wonderful night under their heavy tarp, the only shelter they had, a night of conversation about different cultures and places and a night of magnificent fiddle music. There was nothing like the Adirondacks, they told us, in their native land—the vastness, complexity, and emptiness of this place was beyond their experience. They were clearly intoxicated with it.

Another fall outing from Blue Mountain Lake to Axton remains unclassified in my personal canoe trip file. It was a leisurely, week-long outing with my perennial canoeing partner, Jim. This was the perfect trip, or so we thought. The weather, although cool, was sunny throughout. Fall colors were peaking, wildlife was everywhere, and we never had to compete with another soul for lean-tos. Jim's stiff back was bothering him, but because we were not in a hurry, it wasn't a serious problem.

On the seventh day, we pulled in alongside the boat-launch site off Route 3 where we had left our car. Jim grabbed the retaining wall and pulled us close in. We exchanged comments on how this had truly been one of the great trips. Then Jim stood up in the bow, his back suddenly had a spasm, and, with a disbelieving look at me over his shoulder, he slowly toppled backwards into the river. He submerged completely, taking much of the gear in the front of the canoe with him. Somehow, I managed not to go over, but our craft took on a good two feet of water and I was wet to my waist.

Jim managed to pull himself ashore. We rescued the floating gear and hauled the canoe into the parking lot and dumped the water out. By this time, Jim was shaking uncontrollably. The water was frigid, he was tired and his back was still bad. He was showing real signs of hypothermia. We stripped him off in the lot, got dry clothes on him from the waterproof bag, and put him in the car for twenty minutes with the heater on full blast before he could finally stop the shivering.

Although that certainly ranks among my most exasperating finishes, for sheer frustration I have never found anything to surpass missing the turnoff below Axton and having to make that endless journey around the Oxbow. The main channel of the Raquette makes a sharp cut through a small opening along the shore. It is easy to miss. If you don't know exactly where you are on the river, I suppose you could travel around and around that looping oxbow, like some sort of Rushton Van Winkle, for twenty years. Thank God I did it only once. After a long and exhausting day, that added distance is enough to make even the most inexperienced map reader improve his skills.

Nowadays we limit our travels on this chain to early spring or late fall. So many Adirondack rivers are off-limits as a result of posting, we have found the route much too crowded for our liking in the summer.

One memorable trip in early July, we arrived at our starting point at the hamlet of Raquette Lake to find a group of at least thirty boy scouts in some fifteen canoes. Many had hit the water an hour or two ahead of us, and others continued to pack gear and prepare even as we pushed off. For four interminable days, we were surrounded by this boisterous group. Their singing and loud laughter and clanking paddles on aluminum canoes never left us. All the prime campsites were taken, all the wildlife scared away, all the firewood consumed.

Through it all, I tried to remind myself that it was good for youngsters to enjoy the river. I had certainly done the same at their age, and it was no doubt the foundation for my later love of the out-of-doors. Yet I continue to believe to this day that groups should in some way be limited from such enormous sizes.

Finally, we are at the foot of the lake. It has taken us four hours of continuous paddling in the face of that wind. My shoulders and arms feel like they are on fire. We stake our claim to one of the lean-tos just inside the entrance to the river and, as if to laugh at us, the wind immediately dies away and the lake surface grows still.

Jim shakes his head and stomps off to look for firewood. I stand at the water's edge and listen to the sudden silence. For hours, the noise of wind, slapping waves, and grunting exertion has filled the day. Now I just listen. I can hear the river waiting for us. A final breath of air ripples along its dark surface and disappears. A break in the clouds sprouts sudden rays of golden sunlight, and the entire setting seems to admonish, "Such a fuss over a little wind."

I nod and smile a little. No, the trick the elements have played on us this day cannot ruin my mood, for ahead of us lies what no rain, wind, or endless oxbows, no throngs of boy scouts or sudden cold dunkings can ever dilute. Ahead lies the beauty and solitude of a wild river.

Autumn

Autumn is the season of essence here in the North Country. It is what people enjoy most about this golden place between the high mountains and the big river. It is about auburn fields of corn alternating with dark spatters of spruce, sugar maples outlining red dairy barns, windy days, and bulbous clouds chasing shadows across a rolling landscape.

It is about college football games, children playing in leaf piles, country auctions, and fresh apple cider. It is about long walks down quiet country roads past two-hundred-year old stone fences and overgrown foundations redolent with history. And it is about storm windows, getting the firewood in, and digging out winter clothing.

Most of all, it is about color. Winter is white, though less so, if our elders are to be believed, than was once the case. Spring, before the buds break forth, is all black and white, snow and mud and empty tree branches. Summer is green, of course, bare feet and newly mown lawns. But in the fall, the monochromatic scheme gives way and the result lifts the spirit.

For some, the red and orange of the maple epitomize this time of year; blood-red splashes of color ripple across the Adirondack foothills, giving every landscape the feel of inspired canvas. The colors blaze briefly and then die in what seems an orgy of waste. But, as Richard Jefferies, the 19th century chronicler of English rural life once wrote, "there is no economy, thrift, or saving, in nature; it is one splendid waste. It is that waste which makes it so beautiful, and so irresistible!"

But of all the season's colors, it is the bronze of autumn that truly glorifies the Northlands. Who could ever imagine so many elaborations on a single theme? Every field sports its own hue, every barn weathers to a different shade. Each cornfield browns at its own pace dependent only upon differing factors of soil content, elevation, or exposure.

During autumn, the North Country feels both whole and timeless. The same elements repeat, yet we never grow tired of them. Admit it, summer becomes wearisome by late August and spring is mere transition—the Gerry Ford of seasons. For too many, winter is only to be escaped from—where is their sense of place? To experience the essence of fall, they must know winter as well.

Each season has its patrons, and justly so. But only autumn offers such variety of landscape, of weather, of "color." The same every year, yet always glorious, uplifting, elating. Who could ever call this season monotonous? The artist may as well call his palette boring.

"We get only transient and partial glimpses of the beauty of the world," Thoreau wrote. Surely, a North Country autumn must be one of those glimpses.

Cranberry Lake

I have been afloat on Cranberry Lake no more than an hour or two but have nonetheless spent many weeks on its waters. There is really not much of a riddle here. This third-largest lake in the Adirondacks often sports winds that are uninviting to paddlers. Yet its waters rise deep in the Five Ponds Wilderness, where the snakelike Oswegatchie River winds its way to join the lake at Wanakena. The Oswegatchie trip to High Falls and beyond is a favorite of many Adirondack river-lovers, and it is there that I spent so much time on the "future" waters of Cranberry Lake.

Shaped something like an octopus, the lake has at least seven or eight arms of varying width. Over a century ago, it was almost doubled in size by the construction of a dam. As the waters rose, they backed up the long arms of feeder streams, thus giving the lake its distinctive shape. Also flooded and sent packing into the history books were the cranberry bogs that had given the lake its name.

Cranberry Lake is one of the most beautiful bodies of water in the Adirondacks, largely because its shoreline is primarily state-owned and classified wild forest or wilderness. It is surrounded by summits ranging up to twenty-six hundred feet in height. At one time, the lake was renowned for having one of the best brook trout fisheries in the Northeast. But the introduction of competing species such as yellow perch, combined with a warming of the waters as a result of the dam, led to the decline of the trout.

Initially very remote, the lake has survived to the present day in better shape than many others. Not until the advent of the automobile did man finally begin to make his distinctive mark. According to Albert Fowler, in his book *Cranberry Lake—From Wilderness to Adirondack Park,* the earliest settlers arrived a full generation or more after others had reached Raquette and Long Lakes, the Saranacs, and the lakes of the Fulton chain. Lumbering was also slow to gain a foothold. Loggers arrived in the Saranacs and along the Raquette River in the 1850s, but they did not reach Cranberry until the 1890s.

Verplanck Colvin, the Adirondack surveyor, reported on the wilderness south of Cranberry Lake in 1874. The following year, William H. H. Murray, whose *Adventures in the Wilderness* had sparked thousands of sportsmen to visit the Adirondacks, paid a visit to the lake. Rumors of fantastic fishing on virgin trout waters soon were making the rounds.

In short order, stories of the fishing began to appear in magazines like *Field and Stream.* Sportsmen and tourists had finally discovered the beautiful and remote waters of Cranberry Lake. Among them was Frederic Remington, who spent part of almost every summer during the 1890s in the area. Using the Rasbeck brothers as guides, Remington explored far and wide and produced many fine illustrations and paintings.

In 1892, Remington traveled by canoe from Cranberry Lake down the Oswegatchie as far as Gouverneur, where his trip was abruptly halted by the spring drive of logs that reached from bank to bank. His craft for this trip was a sixteen-foot cedar canoe called the *Necoochee.* It had probably been purchased in Canton from his good friend J. Henry Rushton.

Not far from where the Oswegatchie enters the lake on Inlet Flow is the Forest Technology campus of the State University of New York at Wanakena, otherwise known as the New York State Ranger School. The tiny but picturesque village of Wanakena began its existence as a lumbering town. By 1912, however, the Rich Lumber Company had cut most of the virgin timber and moved on. The Ranger School was established, in part, to help the town's ailing economy.

Today, one can stand in the hamlet of Cranberry Lake and stare out at distant shores that are still green and inviting. The lake remains one of the jewels of the Adirondack Park.

Canoe Brawl

I've rarely met a paddler I couldn't like or at least get along with. There is something about the commonality of experience that seems to make such people appreciative and protective of the out-of-doors. And that tends to make them people that I can find common ground with.

So it was with a certain amount of shock that I read an account in the *Lewiston (Maine) Sun-Journal* that was headlined: "Canoe Brawl Began on Sand-bar."

Canoe Brawl.

The placing of those two words side by side seems an almost inconceivable contradiction. But there it was. The unlikely event occurred on Maine's Saco River. The Saco happens to be a historic river. It was here that one of the country's first sawmills was located way back in the 1600s.

Now the Saco has a new claim to fame. The section near Fryeburg where the brawl took place has as many as four thousand canoeists on an average summer weekend. I've never experienced being on a river with four thousand other canoe enthusiasts—thank God. Maybe if I had, I just might have been in the mood for a brawl myself.

The altercation apparently occurred when one group of six canoeists tried to intervene when members of a larger group tipped over the canoe of an elderly couple. Thirty-two youths, comprising only "part" of the larger group, then attacked members of the smaller group with beer bottles and paddles. To escape, some of the attacked group ran into the woods. They called police, who responded with fifteen officers. The net result was one arrest, eleven others issued summonses, and seven taken to a hospital for injuries ranging up to broken ribs.

Such incidents are apparently not uncommon on the Saco. In 1987, state police and liquor commission officials began a crackdown that included "searching" canoes for illegal substances. On Memorial Day weekend alone, seventy-eight cases of beer and drugs including cocaine, crack, and marijuana were confiscated, and twenty-seven men were arrested.

In 1988, the Maine Civil Liberties Union challenged the searches, and the following year, the state Supreme Court ruled that the searches were illegal.

I've had a hard time trying to decide how I feel about all of this. I'm not fond of free rein for police searches, and the idea of being stopped and searched by police while canoeing appalls me. The whole point of the canoeing experience is to get away from people— to enjoy the carefree freedom of the wilderness. The only thing I want to see around the next bend is a moose—not a police checkpoint.

But clearly, canoeists congregating in groups of four thousand are not looking for a transcending wilderness experience. As I've already said, I have rarely come across a rowdy group of canoeists. Yet it has happened a time or two, and I was angry enough at the loss of my own solitude to have wished for a policeman to turn to. The bottom line is, I simply cannot conceive of being part of a group of four thousand canoeists any more than I could conceive of the words "Canoe Brawl" being headlined in a newspaper.

What's the answer? Backcountry permit systems have been instituted in some parks, but they are widely resisted and are nearly impossible to enforce in a park as vast as the Adirondacks. But more such controls will almost certainly become necessary—at least in selected areas as popular as the Saco—as pressures build on our fewer and fewer remaining wild areas.

Just Folks

As I prepare for my annual sea kayaking trip to Nova Scotia, I have been trying to explain to a relative what it is like to be in a kayak and on the ocean. He is a sailor—an enthusiast of the high seas himself. Yet there is a difference, a gulf between our experiences.

I have never cared much for sailing. Admittedly, my experience is limited. I also have a tendency to get seasick. But the bottom line is that the idea of spending days on end with nothing to see but the horizon strikes me as being on a par with bicycling across the flat fields of Denmark, something I had the "opportunity" to do when I was nineteen. In one sense, that outing was not unlike sailing. A relentless wind was in my face the entire two weeks. Though the terrain was flat, the steady gusting winds made every stroke of the pedal an effort. I pored over the maps trying to set a course that might defeat the wind. I was never successful. It seemed that even when I stopped and turned my bike around and headed back the way I had come, that relentless wind turned with me. I took to wondering what ancient Danish gods I must somehow have offended.

Of course, one doesn't have to sail on the open ocean. Cruising through the Greek Islands or even our own Thousand Islands is no doubt an enjoyable pastime. But the freedom and the closeness to nature that come with sea kayaking, or canoeing, for that matter, strike me as far more enjoyable than sailing. In a kayak that draws, at most, a few inches of water, there is virtually no place that you cannot go. Every little cove and inlet can be explored. A glance over the side reveals another world of sea grasses, shimmering scallop shells, intricate rock formations, and multicolored fish. The spits, half-moon cob-

Sea kayaking—adventure for the entire family.

bled beaches, craggy points, and cormorant-covered islets that I can
explore with abandon represent primarily danger to the sailor, who
fears for his hull.

So sailors remain somewhat distanced from their surroundings.
They must always keep to the center of the channel and must always
be looking for possible shallows. Maybe that's why so many sailors
have regaled me about the wonders of the open sea. No doubt, that is
where they feel the safest. Just imagine it, they insist, the salt spray in
your face, the rise and fall with the swell, those incredible sunsets.

Well, I'm closer to the salt spray in my kayak than they are and
that rise and fall with the swell only reminds me of the lunch I've just
eaten that is rising and swelling within. And as for sunsets? I've seen
plenty, and I've yet to see one sinking into the emptiness of the sea
that could hold a candle to a sun setting against the backdrop of a
sparkling cove studded with islands. Give me a backdrop any day.

It's simply that I like to look at things. My favorite canoeing is on
the tiniest of streams because every bend brings an entirely new set of
backdrops. It is like watching the ever-changing variety of a nature
special on TV. Would you sit in front of a TV screen that never

changed—that showed the same line where sky and water meet and nothing else?

Not to belabor the point. I like sailors. Sailors seem to me to be very nice people. I once stood on a headland above the Bosporus in Istanbul and watched Onassis's yacht, complete with Jackie Kennedy on deck, sail beneath me. I waved to them. They waved back.

Sailors. Just folks. Like you and me.

Indian Summer

A recent weekend marked the most beautiful Indian summer days that I can remember and, for once, my timing was perfect. My canoeing partner and I listened to weather reports all week. As usual, they changed daily if not hourly. As late as Thursday night, we considered putting off our trip because the reports were calling for rain all three days.

But I resisted. I am no longer willing to plan outings around weather reports. Unless a major weather system is descending, that is, an all-points bulletin, force five hurricane with spin-off tornados, and the odd earthquake, I refuse to listen. Experience suggests they are right no more than 50 percent of the time. And nothing—NOTHING—is more painful than to sit at home after canceling a trip and watch a weekend like the last one unfold with little to do but clean out the barn.

Besides, the truth is, some of the most rewarding canoe trips I have had have been on rainy, misty, or foggy days when the light can be perfect for photography and when even the occasional thunderstorm has its compensations.

So there we were on that perfect Indian summer weekend simply luxuriating down one piece of wet wilderness and up another. We canoed part or all of Lake Lila, Shingle Shanty Creek, Beaver River, Stony Creek Ponds, Stony Creek, the Raquette River, the Osgood River, and Lake Meacham. We gorged ourselves on some of the most spectacular fall colors either of us could remember.

On Lake Lila, we saw only a handful of other paddlers. We were regaled, however, with a few of those sounds that one almost never

On many Adirondack rivers, paddling upstream requires lifting over innumerable beaver dams.

seems to be completely free of in modern society. The background hum and roar of planes seemed nearly continuous. There was a distant but thoroughly disturbing chain saw reverberating across the hills. And on this first weekend of muzzle-loading season, the rumbling thump of the guns was steady.

Still, there is a feeling of remoteness to this Adirondack lake, the largest to be completely surrounded by state-owned land. I particularly like the "procession of the pines," that stately line that the soaring trees make as they march along the top of an esker. The windblown pines tower above their lesser neighbors, the spruce, birch, and cedar, at regular intervals all around the lake, providing plentiful spots for nesting osprey. The white pine is my favorite tree, and there are few better places to see them in all their glory. As we paddled down Beaver River outlet, magnificent whites towered against the sky or leaned away over the river, encouraging us to make haste beneath them.

On the Raquette River, downstream from Stony Creek, we paddled up Follensby Pond outlet as far as the first posted signs. Here, more than 130 years ago, Alfred B. Street wrote, "The sunlight lay like a golden mantle on the meadow." Distant mountains and the same magnificent open vistas beckoned to us as well. But we resisted the temptation to proceed—for now. The purchase of the lake is still being somewhat tentatively negotiated by the state, and this hardly seems the time to alienate its owner.

Other things have changed since Alfred Street's day. As his group pulled ashore at the entrance to Follensby, he wrote, "The cheerful hack of the axe was echoing as we landed." Hardly the sort of thing that today's concerned paddlers are inclined to wax poetic about. On the other hand, in those pre–L. L. Bean days, the sound of that axe heralded felled saplings to make a shelter and spruce boughs for beds—deep woods amenities that would go a long way toward making the sound of an axe a "cheerful" one.

The Dismal Wilderness

The word "Adirondack" is a romantic and primitive one, seemingly indicative of a place once replete with early Americans living in harmony with the land. Surely, Native Americans lived here, constructed their villages, used ancient hunting sites, and revered sacred battlegrounds.

Not so. The mountain realm was in fact nearly deserted before the arrival of the white man. The Adirondacks were only occasionally used by the Indians either as a travel route or as a hunting grounds. To be sure, there was usually good hunting in the mountains, and both the Algonquins of Canada and the Mohawks of the Five Nations to the south used the region extensively for this purpose. But neither travel nor hunting leave much in the way of physical evidence. Outside of a very few artifacts, the Indians provided us with little sign of their passing.

Following Samuel de Champlain's voyage up the St. Lawrence and Richelieu Rivers to Adirondack soil near Ticonderoga in 1609, Jesuit missionaries and trappers were among the earliest white men to visit the region. They began their work with the Mohawks as early as the 1640s. Father Jogues may have been the first European to see Lake George, albeit as a tortured captive of the Iroquois in 1642. Later, the profitable beaver pelt business brought the French, Dutch, and Indians into the Adirondacks. William Chapman White, in his classic book, *Adirondack Country*, relates the story of a wheelwright in Malone who discovered a bullet embedded in an old Adirondack log. The ring count of the wood showed that the bullet had been fired two hundred years before, in about 1650.

State geologist Ebenezer Emmons christened the region "the Adirondacks" in 1837. Prior to this, there were many Indian names, their meanings often lost to the ages. According to Thomas Pownall in 1784, the Iroquois may have called the region *Couchsachrage,* which has been translated as "The Place of Winter," "The Dismal Wilderness," "The Beaver Hunting Grounds" and "The Place of the Beaver Dams." The earliest map of the area, in 1570, labeled all of northern New York "Avocal," a term whose meaning has been lost.

The arrival of the white man did not simplify things. An English map of 1761 simply called the region "Deer Hunting Country." Some maps called it "Iroquoisia." Other terms used included "The Mountains of Saint Marthe," "The Mohegan Mountains," "The Black Mountains," "Clinton's Mountains," after De Witt Clinton, "Macomb's Mountains," after the land speculator, and "The Aganushioni Range," after the Iroquois word for longhouse. Some early Frenchmen called the place "The Peru Mountains." Downstaters in the 1800s called it "The Great Northern Wilderness" or simply "The North Woods."

According to many sources, "Adirondacks" is authentic Iroquois, supposedly a term of derision for the Algonquins, who lived off tree bark during hard winters. But this has been disputed. One scholar thought "Adirondacks" was derived from a tribe living in the lower St. Lawrence in the 1500s and meant "They of the Great Rocks." The Iroquois may then have picked it up, mistranslating it to "They Who Eat Trees." To finally complicate matters, a Mohawk vocabulary compiled in 1634 by Dutch traders marked the first appearance of the word "Aderondacke" in print and was used to mean "Frenchmen and Englishmen."

With today's new appreciation for our fast-disappearing wild places, "The Dismal Wilderness" simply won't do. And we can thank our stars that "Macomb's Mountains" never caught on. The ancient mountains of New York richly deserve their romantic name, molded from legend and hard wilderness reality alike.

Generators and Loons

At the end of Low's Lake, at the end of the day, in one of the remotest parts of New York State, my companion and I sit in our canoe and listen to the most extraordinary loon concert we have ever heard. The serenade is apparently set off by a float plane that roars in low over our heads and then slowly disappears across the hills. The moment the plane's hum dissipates, the birds begin to call. It is as if they need to reassure each other that they are not alone after the traumatic event of the plane's passing.

And so they call to each other. I've experienced other such loon recitals. One of the finest was off the Nova Scotia coast in early evening as my companion and I floated soundlessly in our sea kayaks. But even that marvelous concert hardly compares with what we hear now on Low's Lake, for the birds appear eager to outdo one another in the intricacies of their lilting calls. They seem, literally, to be experimenting with the limits of their vocal range. It is one of the grandest moments I've had in the wild.

Later, as we sit having dinner, looking out over the lake, someone starts up a generator beyond the hills. It makes a steady hum, is loud enough to be irritating, and is destined, we eventually learn, to go on for hours. It hardly seems possible that we have come all this way only to be serenaded by an engine—especially after our encounter with the loons.

I begin to wonder if the sound will continue all night. I always have trouble sleeping the first two or three nights in the woods. My theory is it's because I need time to let my body decompress from society. The quiet of the woods is so different from the night sounds

Low's Lake in the Bog River wilderness.

of my village home that it often keeps me awake. But this night the generator does, in fact, hum on into the wee hours and, lulled by its similarity to the hums of home, I sleep like a baby.

I spend part of the evening reading Bill McKibben's book, *The Age of Missing Information*, in which he describes his thoughts and feelings as he watches one thousand hours of television—the total offering from a single cable system's scores of channels during one twenty-four-hour period. It strikes me as odd to be away from the incessant presence of the tube and yet to be reading a book about it. In fact, I am in the perfect position to identify with what McKibben is trying to do, for in the book, he contrasts his thousand-hour day with another of the twenty-four-hour variety that he spent climbing an Adirondack mountain.

It is a book full of insights that I hardly have room to explore here, but McKibben has done all of us TV watchers a bit of a favor, I think, by actually admitting—right there in print—that he watched a thousand hours of mind-numbing television. Most of us spend a lot of time declaring that "we" hardly watch any TV at all. Then along comes an actual intellectual who tells us he did little else for months. I found McKibben's admission liberating, though this is hardly the effect, I hasten to add, that the author was after.

Nature shows on TV, McKibben tells us, rarely inspire such reflection. "The nature documentaries are as absurdly action-packed as the soap operas. . . . Trying to understand 'nature' from watching Wild Kingdom is as tough as trying to understand 'life' from watching *Dynasty*."

Clearly, it's better to be out here in the real wilderness, even if the generators do, occasionally, compete with the loons.

River Without End

For all its size and importance, the St. Lawrence River is sometimes overlooked by those of us more drawn to the varied waters of the Adirondacks. I am as guilty of this as anyone. Though I have traveled the St. Lawrence by ferry, sailboat, and even ocean liner, I have never dipped my paddle blade in her.

I have been reminded of this error of omission by friends who have paddled in the Thousand Islands and also by accounts of the superb kayaking and whale sighting to be had off the river's north shore near the Mingan Islands.

The length and size of the river is difficult to determine precisely. Does it actually begin only once its channel leaves Lake Ontario and enters the bay of the Thousand Islands, or is its ultimate source really the little river St. Louis, which rises near the head of the Mississippi and drains into Lake Superior? Does it cease to be a true river below Quebec City, at which point the water is no longer entirely fresh, or is it essentially a river all the way to the Gaspé Peninsula where the St. Lawrence meets the sea? The Indians, after all, called this place *gaspeg*, literally, the "end of the world." Thus, it would seem a fitting spot for the end of a great river as well.

Regardless, the St. Lawrence River basin remains the third largest in North America with an area of some 365,000 square miles. If one includes the area of the five Great Lakes, this dimension increases by another 95,000 square miles. Without doubt, the St. Lawrence is one of the world's largest inland transportation avenues.

It is also the gateway to an entire continent. Native Americans used it to delineate boundaries between the various tribes and fished

Junction of the Ottawa and St. Lawrence Rivers. Adirondack timber was lashed into rafts and floated to markets in Montreal. Steel engaving from Canadian Scenery *(London: Willis and Bartlett, 1842).*

its bounteous waters through the ages. When the white man came, the river became a highway of exploration. Jacques Cartier, the Pathfinder; Samuel de Champlain, the Father of French colonization; and Count Louis de Baude Frontenac, the Savior of New France, were among the more prominent to attach their names forever to the great concourse.

The St. Lawrence has been largely responsible for the way the white man dealt with the new world. There was the age of the fur trade and the voyageur, the empire of the timber barons who floated huge log rafts down the great river, the coming of hydropower and the rise of manufacturing, and, finally, the transformation brought about by the International Seaway, which conquered the rapids and allowed ocean-going vessels access to the interior of the continent.

A river of so many varied parts can never be fully explored by any one person. Yet, as paddlers, we could scarcely be more perfectly located than here at the edge of the Thousand Islands. In truth, a thousand lifetimes might be pleasurably spent in exploring the river and its islands, not to mention its many tributaries and the amazing inland waterway of connecting lakes, rivers, and canals that runs from Kingston north to Ottawa and beyond.

It was a river that seemed to connect with everything of watery importance in the new world. Indeed, when Cartier inquired of one of his two captured native pilots: "What river is this?" the man solemnly replied: "A river without end."

Fall Outing Trio

I am an unabashed lover of streams. Given a choice, I will always choose the small, meandering stream over a large river or lake. Impounded waters behind dams are not, therefore, amongst my favorite places to go. All one has to do is read David Brower's description of what was lost behind the Glen Canyon Dam and he will never feel ambivalent about such things again. Even a man as committed as Brower can have his off days, however, and he readily admits that he might have stopped that particular dam if he had but taken a stronger stance. He writes that he has never forgiven himself for that inertia.

Which is all a roundabout way of excusing myself to you out-of-the-way wilderness paddlers for finding myself on the impounded waters of the Raquette River. With two free hours, I am unable to resist a jaunt midst the islands of the Raquette in the village of Potsdam. This is truly a "dammed" beautiful bit of river with a host of features that make it attractive.

Fall colors are peaking, and the islands and shoreline are replete with brilliant maple trees. It is a spectacular colorfest. The many little islands and peninsulas make this relatively small area fascinating to examine. There are endless ins and outs, and one can easily spend half a day exploring. It is even possible to get a bit of a workout paddling up the channel to the dam depending on how much water is being released.

I see no other boats during my two hours and only two other people—a young couple sitting on a log by the shore, kissing. That sight seems only too appropriate for a lovely fall day and does not diminish my feelings of solitude.

It is hard to believe sometimes that there can be so much to see right under our noses. I spend a good deal of time in Potsdam, generally unaware of the many living things that make their homes here—other than humans, that is. Today, ducks and geese are everywhere. I keep surprising them as I meander into yet another winding pass between islets. A large osprey lifts from the top of a towering white pine and continues to hover above me until I move on.

As I paddle up the shore past the graveyard with its pearl-white stones contrasting starkly with the blazing red and orange maples, I spy what appears to be the outlet of a stream. Making my way over to it, I enter a channel rich with fall color. One turn leads to another, enticing me farther into the woods. Finally, I come to the end in a quiet pool. I cease paddling and float soundlessly toward the woods, drinking in the colors. Suddenly, my boat hits a submerged twig and a sharp sound penetrates the silence. Immediately in front of me, an almost perfectly camouflaged owl leaves its perch and flies heavily into the woods, clearly annoyed at my intrusion.

In the Adirondack foothills, I take advantage of another easily accessible North Country paddle. Even though the day is blisteringly hot and muggy, the first traces of fall color are visible during an Adirondack Mountain Club outing on Massawepie Lake. Our group paddles about the beautiful little lake and down the outlet for a mile or two. The tiny stream meanders aimlessly as it works its way into Massawepie Mire, eventually connecting with the South Branch of the Grass River.

The Massawepie Lake tract is owned by the Otetiana Council of Boy Scouts. The lake is off-limits to boaters when the scouts are in residence—from the last week in June to the last week in August. But the rest of the time, the public is welcome, and there is a register by the side of the road to sign going in.

The lake sits amidst a pristine bowl of low hills. At one end are a pair of twin eskers, one of which bisects two long and narrow bays. The entrances to these bays are undetectable until you are practically upon them. It is easy to imagine the scouts playing endless games of Indians and explorers here. The shores are lined with large white and red pine, the forest floor a soft and deep carpet formed by centuries of their fallen needles. Follow the trail inside the entrance to the second bay and you come to Pine Pond, a landlocked and lonely pool that can easily be circumnavigated on foot. I once came upon a pair of early morning fishermen sitting quietly in their small rowboat here, appearing and disappearing magically as the morning mist alternately engulfed and revealed them.

Osprey are nesting just inside one of the twin bays. I suspect I saw these very birds when I made this trip in the spring and wonder if they might even be the same ones Paul Jamieson mentions seeing in his guidebook back in 1979, more than a decade ago. Once inside the first of the long bays, our various crafts spread out, floating peacefully in the bowl-like dead end when a pair of loons begin to call. The birds appear completely at ease with our presence, and it is mystical to float, listening to the variations of their cries as they resound in the little bowl of trees and water.

Dick Tiel and I hike away from the main group after our lunch break to explore one of the narrow eskers that divide the bays. An esker is formed by a glacial stream of meltwater that washes the various gravels out of the ice sheet. The deposits build up higher and higher, often following the meandering course of the stream for miles.

It is a beautiful place to hike, the aging forest of pine offering open vistas on every front. From the highest point, we peer down on water all around us and have a superb view of the outlet stretching away in the distance. Here, the boys have been busy. A full-growth white pine trunk, fallen perhaps half a century ago, has been carefully perched at the apex of the esker. It forms a perfect teeter-totter at least fifty feet in length. We try it out, of course. Dick was once a scout after all, and I can make claim to having been a Cub Scout for a week when I was eleven. I might have stayed on if I'd known teeter-tottering was part of the course.

We are just getting the rhythm when we hear voices approaching. The scouts? No. But a group of young girls is hiking up the trail. They stop to call out to a sailboat in the bay, and we make a quiet retreat. Old scouts are not what interests them.

On still another day, I cast my craft into the waters of Brandy Brook outside of Madrid. This unassuming little stream meanders out of a large wetland one would never guess was there from the highway. About half an hour upstream after crossing four or five beaver dams, a railroad bed splits the marsh like a knife blade. Scrambling up the rise, I view the entire wetland basin. It is a spot worthy of a modest lunch, taken while watching a large flock of geese soar high overhead, their cries reverberating like conversation at a particularly raucous cocktail party.

As I paddle away, a train whistle sounds. Sure enough, a few minutes later, the train appears. It is hauling three passenger cars, and as the engineer slows to negotiate the rickety bridge, thirty people are suddenly waving at me.

An unexpected encounter, certainly, but one that leaves me with a good feeling. Where else but in the North Country can one find so much readily accessible canoeing?

Gargoyles in Paradise

Mid-November and here I am kayaking down the center of Highland Lake in New Hampshire on what must surely be the last perfect weekend of this extraordinarily mild autumn.

If I close my eyes and paddle rhythmically, I can almost believe I am in the Adirondacks. We flush a huge congregation of Canada geese. They have taken their time calculating if we are a serious enough threat to warrant action. By the time they conclude that we are, only fifty yards separate us, the closest I've been to a really large collection of birds all taking flight at the same time. We can hear their wings beating on the water, and their honking is contentious—how dare we disturb them?

The geese clearly feel the lake belongs to them this time of year. And they plainly are used to humans. For Highland Lake is no Lake Lila, that pristine Adirondack pool totally surrounded by wilderness. Here, magnificent homes line the shores all the way around this seven-mile-long body of water. By rough estimate, I would guess there is a summer population here of thousands of people living in millions of dollars worth of real estate.

Most of the lakes of southern New England are like this, wall-to-wall buildings and people. We can thank our stars that things went along quite differently in the Adirondacks for a century or so, with the rich and famous purchasing entire lakes upon which to build their dream homes and estates. The result is that much of the shorefront in the Adirondacks remained untouched until relatively recently when the modern second-home industry began to make serious inroads on that legacy.

But Highland Lake is quiet today, remarkably so, given the number of homes. Indeed, one of my companions says that he was on the lake in August when it was like being in someone's giant bathtub, the water literally blanketed with motorboats. Radios blared, teenagers screamed, dogs barked, hammers pounded, and chain saws roared. The surface of the lake churned from the myriad motors, and my friend could scarcely glance at the shore or look up at the birds for fear of being run down by the powerboats whizzing around him.

This dazzling Saturday afternoon in mid-November, however, the lake is virtually deserted. During a six-hour paddle the entire length and back again, we pass only two powerboats, two other kayakers, and a lone man sculling. My partner shakes his head and mutters something about how crazy people are not to be here now, when the lake is at its finest, deserted, quiet, and home to many geese, ducks, and other birds.

But these strange folks who build extravagant homes with elaborate boathouses and multiple-layered decks spouting mail-order gargoyles, saunas, and satellite dishes, apparently have no interest at all in being here at any time other than when everyone else is here. Even then, evidently, many of them would prefer to be inside watching the latest satellite feed from New York.

We are surrounded by the conspicuous and successful American capitalist at his finest. See and be seen is the name of this game. It is almost beyond my comprehension, but it nevertheless makes for a quiet and enjoyable afternoon for three impecunious souls.

True Confessions

It may be hard to believe given the depth of snow and ice still covering rivers and streams this harsh winter of 1993–94, but opening day of fishing season in New York State has once again come and gone. This year, I have decided to bite the bullet and come clean on the fishing issue. There are a lot of people out there who may never feel the same about me after I get this off my chest. So be it. I'm feeling bold.

I don't fish.

But wait—that is not the end of it. The fisherperson in the family is my wife. There, the awful truth is revealed.

Over the years, I have grown accustomed to people assuming that I must fish because I love to canoe. And indeed, as a little tyke, I often went fishing off the bridge over the Grass River in Canton. Mind you, I never managed to catch anything exceeding five inches in length, and once I had bagged this diminutive prey, inevitably my reel stopped working, and I would end up with two miles of tangled line that looked like a crate of whip licorice after twelve Cub Scouts fought for shares.

Fishing is not in my blood.

My wife's family, on the other hand, is fiendish about the whole business. They can trace their genealogical lines back through Spencer Tracy in *The Old Man and the Sea* to Captain Ahab and on to that fellow who did something with loaves and fishes. Behind our house is a small pond that my wife stocks with bass. When her family comes to visit, they all troop off with their poles and boots and lures and lucky hats to spend days standing beside this tiny pond catching fish that are, frankly speaking, already a captive audience.

This does not bother me. Lots of people participate in recreational activities that I would rather not participate in. George Bush fires horseshoes, Bill Clinton fires off policy papers, George Steinbrenner fires managers, and so forth. I say, to each his own.

But the sad fact is, fishermen look upon those who do not fish as little better than the lowest forms of slime molds. I am pitied, mocked, slandered, ridiculed, and pilloried. And that is just by my immediate family.

The very idea that someone who actually writes about canoeing should not know the first thing about fishing is greeted as ample grounds for disbarment from the entire enterprise of outdoor writing. And the injustice of it is that I have tried to learn something about the subject just to fend off the onslaught. I own quite a few books about fishing. Mind you, I've never managed to read beyond the first paragraph in any of them without falling asleep. Still, they give me great comfort, and when my wife and her family disappear to commune with the denizens of the deep, I take to my study and stare at the rows of fishbooks and imagine what might have been.

So don't ask my advice about anything having to do with leaders or flies or the Bait Distance Double-Handed 30 g Casting Competition. Don't expect me to be able to explain the difference between bonefish and coho, wahoo and snook. And if you ever invite me to go canoeing and you intend to fish, just prop me up against the nearest outcrop, hand me a cold beer, and leave me be.

Whatever you do, don't insult me. Because that's the one area where I am a certified expert.

Raquette Lake

Raquette Lake is the fourth largest body of water (excluding Lake Champlain) in the Adirondack Park. Shaped rather like an amoeba, its many elongated bays and inlets make it a treat to explore by canoe.

Lumbermen arrived along the shores of Raquette Lake about the time of the Civil War, invading the hunting grounds of famous guides like Mitchell Sabattis, Alvah Dunning, and Charlie Blanchard. In 1879, furthering this violation of the deep woods, William West Durant began to construct Camp Pine Knot on Long Point, marking the end of the era of crude hunting camps and ushering in the age of wilderness luxury. Camp Pine Knot boasted indoor plumbing, a powder room, and banquet hall and was renowned for its fine cuisine and wine cellar. Durant's Marion River Carry Railroad, which connected via Utowana and Eagle Lakes to Blue Mountain Lake, became, with its steamboats, a major travel route for the wealthy, operating from 1900 to 1929. It was the shortest standard gauge railroad in the world and carried as many as eight thousand passengers a year. The locomotive and one of the passenger cars can be viewed today at the Adirondack Museum.

Throughout the 1800s, lumbering progressed steadily up the Raquette River into the mountains as the more easily attainable timber was cut down. In 1850, Dr. Henry Hewitt of Potsdam lobbied the New York State Legislature successfully to pass a law making the river a public highway. Ten thousand dollars was appropriated to improve the channel so that large quantities of logs could be brought to mill. According to Charles W. Bryan, Jr., in his book, *The Raquette—*

Bridge across the channel connecting Blue Mountain Lake and Eagle Lake, built by W. W. Durant in honor of his father in 1891.

River of the Forest, "For half a century, during spring floods, the Raquette was a writhing mass of logs from Raquette Lake to Potsdam, and the neighboring forests echoed the shouts of hundreds of drivers directing the timber harvest to the mills." A century ago, it cost only ten cents to transport a log over this distance of almost ninety miles.

I have an old lumbering map showing the Raquette Lake region in 1900. Color-coded for "merchantable area," virtually the entire shore of the lake beyond a narrow buffer passes under this classification. Most of the tributaries are labeled "natural timber outlets" and the Brandreth Lake Outlet from Brandreth Lake to Forked Lake is marked as having a "good log road already." There are proposed locations for mill yards, bays marked as good storage areas for logs, and sites indicated for flood dams. There was once even a proposal (never acted upon, fortunately) to change the direction of the Raquette River's flow in order to find a way to move logs into the Hudson River tributaries.

Today, much of Raquette Lake's shoreline is privately owned and classified for moderate and low intensity use. But just beyond are vast areas of state-owned Wild Forest as well as the Pigeon Lake and Blue Ridge Wilderness Areas. Despite this comforting backcountry emptiness, however, a quick glance at the Adirondack Park Land Use and Development Plan map reveals the extent to which the shorelines of nearly all of the larger lakes have been encroached upon by man. A mere handful remain completely or mostly protected—Lake Lila, Meacham Lake, much of Cranberry Lake, and the Stillwater Reservoir come to mind.

Signs of man's heavy hand within the Adirondack Park continue to grow. At some point, as happened eventually with those who decried the excesses of the timber industry, there must be some who will have the foresight to say, "Enough is enough!"

Wetlands

As paddlers, we can appreciate the importance of wetlands. It is the vast wetlands associated with the Adirondacks that help provide the excellent canoeing of northern New York. If not for these swamps, bogs, and marshes, the water would run off the land much more rapidly. In such a scenario, paddling would probably not be a viable activity much past spring runoff. But wetlands make this area one of the best three-season meccas for canoeing in the world.

Wetlands fossil deposits indicate that there were long periods in geological time when swamps and marshes covered most of the continents. Indeed, the dinosaurs most likely got much of their food from the Mesozoic wetlands.

The glaciated wetlands that stretch across much of the earth's upper latitudes appeared only in the last two million years or so as a result of the continental ice sheets advancing and receding. The barren and soggy landscape left in their wake was perfectly suited for wetland organisms.

As the glaciers melted, they left behind, in addition to vast amounts of water, a land carved and shaped by their passage. They dammed rivers and dug deep depressions that formed huge lakes. These bodies of water then silted in to form marshes. Or the ice left behind vast deposits of drift that in time formed sloughs, eskers, kames, and kettle holes (deep bogs and pools).

One of the best examples of this in the Adirondacks occurs in the Massawepie Lake area, where the retreating glacier left an almost magical topography carved from the terrain. Here, canoeists can enjoy lakes separated by long, high eskers that provide engrossing hiking with panoramic views of water on both sides.

The glaciated wetlands were natural homelands for waterfowl and wading birds, which quickly colonized the new terrain. Today, some fourteen thousand years after the last glacier receded, potholes throughout North America accommodate 50 percent of the duck population and are home as well to many fur-bearing mammals.

But wetlands are in trouble around the world. Man has been systematically going about the business of draining them at least since the time of the Mediterranean city-states three thousand years ago. Drained wetlands make extremely good soil for crops. In addition, for many centuries, man thought of swamps and marshes as "evil" places that bred disease.

Much of Europe in Roman times consisted of glaciated wetlands. But today, there are only a few dozen wetlands of significant size in all of central Europe. Only Scandinavia and the Soviet Union have any appreciable amounts of wetland remaining. When the Europeans colonized the Americas, they brought along their concept of what a wetland was good for. It was good for draining, period.

Today, over 90 percent of wetlands in Iowa and Illinois are gone. Many creatures now rare or extinct—the trumpeter swans, whooping cranes, and Carolina parakeets—disappeared when the wetlands of the tallgrass prairies and lower Great Lakes were drained. According to the U.S. Fish and Wildlife Service's 1984 National Wetlands Inventory, fully 54 percent of the nation's original wetlands have been drained or filled. Most of this activity was for agriculture, but also for highways, dams, and urban development.

Beginning in the 1940s, the introduction of pesticides brought a new threat to wetlands. As a result of spraying for mosquitos and the agricultural runoff from crops, pesticide residues grew rapidly. By the early 1960s, it was found that the coastal marshes of Long Island contained some thirteen pounds of DDT per acre.

Recently, in northern New York, resistance was high to a program to expand wetland protection. The reason for the opposition came down to a basic mistrust of government and a fear that the tax base would be undermined. The Bush administration proposed new rules governing wetlands under which, according to four different government agency reports, as much as 50 percent of the nation's wetlands could have been opened to development, including large parts of the

Everglades. This never ending push for economic growth may spell the end of viable wetlands.

We would do well to realize how much our very way of life is dependant on the survival of healthy wetlands. Marshes purify sewage effluent more cheaply than treatment plants. Salt marshes produce significant amounts of our seafood. Swamps store water with less evaporation than reservoirs, and wetlands are part of an entire hydrologic system that provides us with safe and reliable supplies of water.

According to the Fish and Wildlife Service, we are losing between 300 and 450 thousand acres of wetlands a year. It is conceivable that within fifty years, virtually all unprotected wetlands will be gone. The pressures on those remaining will be severe. Like our National Parks, wetlands will become islands of wilderness in an urban ocean. As such, they may not survive.

And neither will we.

Politics

Each generation must deal anew with the . . . tendency to prefer short-run profits to long-run necessities.

—JOHN F. KENNEDY

The 78 Percent

Here's a statistic for you—a Gallup Poll found that 78 percent of Americans call themselves environmentalists. Now clearly not all of these people are out there lobbying their congressmen for less lead in their gasoline or climbing water towers to display "Save the Whales" signs like members of Greenpeace.

There is something else going on here, because if that 78 percent figure is even remotely real, how could we have had twelve years of Reagan-Bush—the most antienvironmental administrations this nation has ever seen? What I think is going on is that people in general have become more and more aware of the many environmental problems out there via the media and even via their own personal experience. To most of these people, a clean environment seems like a perfectly sensible idea. They want to breathe good air, swim with their kids at beaches that don't have hypodermic needles floating around, and drink water that won't give them cancer. Reasonable.

But when it comes down to the ballot box, most people tend to vote either their pocketbooks or the latest war fever. They don't make that crucial connection between the polluted streams behind their houses and the leader up on the TV screen. At best, the environment comes in third. In fact, however, environmental issues probably ought to rank first in the sense that they influence all the other problems. Case in point: The Soviet Union. The Soviets covered up the almost unimaginable environmental destruction that they were doing to their own country. For decades, Soviet leaders sold their people on the fantasy that they were a superpower (our own leaders sold us the same fantasy). Each new five-year plan would pave the way to a fabulous future, they promised. With the fall of the Iron Curtain, it was revealed that that future would be a toxic nightmare.

Much the same sort of thing (albeit to a lesser degree) has been going on in this country. Environmental laws and policies have been given short shrift in favor of the powerful interests of big business and the military. The powers that be have spent enormous sums in the effort to convince the public that setting environmental standards will mean lost jobs, lower economic standards of living, and increased defense risks.

The truth is precisely the opposite. A realistic attack on our serious environmental problems now will prevent those problems from overwhelming us later on. And a serious effort to develop environmentally sound ways to meet the challenges of the future will surely open up new markets and new jobs.

One way is forward-looking, taking a bold but realistic approach. The other way is reactionary, maintaining the status quo. One way offers at least the chance that we will get a handle on our problems before it is too late. The other offers no chance at all and is a certain recipe for another Soviet-style disaster.

The Bush administration was fond of saying that the United States did more to protect the environment than any other nation. Even if true, however, that would be nothing to boast about, because we also contribute the lion's share of the consumption and pollution of the planet. To say the United States does plenty already is a little like saying that pro-choice senator Arlen Spector has done plenty for women—never mind about his treatment of Anita Hill during the Clarence Thomas hearings.

The challenge is to somehow make those 78 percent who think of themselves as environmentalists realize what is at stake and how very much we risk. Former New York governor Mario Cuomo, while speaking of the need for legislation to control overdevelopment in the Adirondacks, put it succinctly: "To do nothing is to do harm."

To do nothing in the face of overpopulation, climate change, ozone holes, toxic pollution, and so many other problems, will surely be to do harm.

Bringing Back the Moose

Two of the best places to spot moose in New York State during the summer and fall of 1995 were outside the tiny villages of West Potsdam and Pierrepont, just north of the Adirondack Park in the St. Lawrence River valley. There were reported sightings of a cow and several bull moose in the area, and others, including at least one calf, have been reported in the same region over the past few years.

Yet moose sightings within the Adirondacks remain exceedingly rare, requiring a healthy dose of luck to go along with a knowledge of moose habits and favored habitat, for there are at most two or three dozen of the giants reportedly roaming within the Blue Line. Weighing in at as much as fifteen hundred pounds and standing seven feet high at the shoulder, they are impressive beasts.

Two hundred years ago, moose thrived throughout the Adirondacks. And as late as 1842, James DeKay, state zoologist, noted that moose were still "numerous" in Essex, Hamilton, Herkimer, Franklin, Lewis, and Warren counties.

In the early 1800s in southern Hamilton County, moose were plentiful enough for one Alvah Dunning and his father to report killing as many as five in a day's hunt. Dunning became one of the great Adirondack guides, leading, among others, Verplanck Colvin and W. H. H. "Adirondack" Murray. He was reputed to have killed his first moose at the age of eleven and to have gone on to kill nearly a hundred of the beasts during his lifetime.

But the arrival of loggers, hunters, and trappers led to the rapid demise of moose. The first Adirondack river drive took place in 1813, and the new method of running logs to mill led to a rapid influx of lumbermen. Clearcutting practices destroyed the dense combination of woodlands and wetlands preferred by moose. Early settlers, whether seeking the beasts for their impressive trophy antlers or for the massive amount of meat they offered, found them an easy target.

The story of the final days of the moose in New York State is a sad but well-documented one. Despite widespread knowledge of the species' endangerment, they continued to be hunted mercilessly. Still, Joel T. Headley was able to report from the McIntyre Iron Works in 1846 that the previous winter two Indians killed eighteen moose.

By the 1850s, moose had only a few strongholds left in the Adirondacks. One was in the remote and rarely visited region at the source of the Bog River. Another encompassed the area around Raquette Lake. Almost every moose seen or killed in the creature's last decade in New York State was recorded in these two locations.

The last known original stock moose was killed in August 1861 by Ransom Palmer of Long Lake, a guide. The moose, a large cow, was shot a few hundred yards upstream from the mouth of the Marion River. The killing was reported to *Forest and Stream* by E. C. Smith, who was a member of the hunting party. In later years, there ensued a heated argument over who could claim to have actually killed the last moose, with Alvah Dunning disputing Palmer's claim in favor of his own. It was perhaps a fitting end to the whole sordid business in an era before anyone thought anything at all about endangered species.

In 1869, nearly a decade after the last moose was seen, the state legislature closed the hunting season on moose. A few years later, in 1874, Verplanck Colvin, the Adirondack surveyor, reported signs and other indications of moose. But for all intents and purposes, moose were considered gone from the state by the time of the Civil War.

About the turn of the century, efforts were made on a number of fronts to reintroduce moose. According to Tom Kalinowski in his excellent article, "Return of the Moose" in the August 1990 issue of *Adirondack Life,* from 1894 to 1903 William Seward Webb released a small number of moose on his private estate, Nehasane Park, in northern Hamilton and Herkimer counties. The Litchfield family, owners of a large preserve south of Tupper Lake, released nineteen of the animals in 1897–98. And the state of New York released six cows and six bulls north of Raquette Lake in 1902.

For a variety of reasons, none of these early efforts was successful. Poaching took a heavy toll. Hunting laws were a new concept at the turn of the century, and many residents living in remote areas simply ignored them. In 1903, 12,000 acres burned in Nehasane Park, part of a series of wide-ranging forest fires that burned 465,000 acres throughout the Adirondacks. It is likely a number of moose perished in the flames.

But most destructive of all to these early moose reintroductions was probably the presence of *Parelaphostrongylus tenius,* or brainworm. Also known as P.t., the worm is carried by white-tailed deer, which acquire it by eating infected snails or slugs. Harmless to the deer, the parasite is eventually expelled, and, if it is then eaten by moose while browsing, the results can be devastating, as it attacks the nervous system. The infected moose loses its motor coordination and perceptual abilities. Death is nearly always the result. It will never be known for certain if P.t. was ultimately responsible for the disappearance of moose from these early stocking programs.

From 1936 through 1979 some twenty moose are believed to have entered New York from Vermont and Canada. Only two were recorded leaving the state. The rest either were shot illegally or simply vanished. From this and from studies in the 1960s, it was concluded that reintroduction of moose to the Adirondacks would not be possible because P.t. was widespread in the deer population.

But in 1980, a moose was sighted near Deer River Flow in the northern Adirondacks. The same year, a half dozen more apparently wandered into northern New York. Within a few years, they were joined by others to form a total of about twenty. These animals thrived despite the presence of brainworm.

Thus encouraged, New York State began the lengthy process of planning a moose reintroduction program. Under Alan Hicks, senior wildlife biologist with the Department of Environmental Conservation's Moose Restoration Project, an environmental impact statement on the reintroduction of moose was released. Hicks believed their findings looked promising. He pointed to the state of Michigan, which introduced a total of 69 moose from 1985 to 1987. Despite some losses, that program flourished with a population in 1990 of 144. This seemed to bode well for the ability of moose to withstand the parasite problems.

A number of statewide public hearings were held on New York's moose reintroduction. Depending on how large a program was undertaken, it was estimated that a viable moose population of as many as thirteen hundred could populate the state within twenty years. The DEC proposal put forth to the public in the summer of 1992 called for financing through voluntary contributions to a special fund, as had been done successfully with the reintroduction of the falcon and the bald eagle. Thus the thorny issue of state funding during a time of budgetary crisis would be circumvented.

Today, moose inhabit the coniferous forests of Canada and Alaska and the northern fringes of many states. Once in danger of extinction in Vermont, New Hampshire, and Maine, moose have made a comeback as forest regrowth replaces disappearing farmland. With the return of the denser forest, the deer population has declined or moved away to areas where meadows and woods meet, their preferred habitat, and fewer deer mean fewer parasites fatal to moose.

Maine estimates its current moose population at twenty-one thousand. New Hampshire has more than four thousand, Vermont about eight hundred. Although most moose inhabit the northern half of the three states, there are signs that they have begun to expand their range. Several years ago, a moose was found on the roof of a factory in Manchester, New Hampshire, a city of more than ninety thousand people. It had climbed an embankment to reach the roof and was unfortunately killed in a fall while people were attempting to rescue it.

One of the greatest threats to moose is also a threat to man—the meeting of the two along highways. Striking a deer can cause considerable damage to a vehicle and kills about 130 people in the United States every year. But hitting a fifteen-hundred-pound animal is a moose of a different color.

The long legs of moose hold them above the beam of most headlights. As a result, their eyes do not cast a reflective light as do those of deer. An auto will simply plow through a moose's legs, allowing the three-quarter-ton body to crash head-on into the windshield. Moose are also notoriously unpredictable. They are attracted to roadside salt deposits, and in the spring, when they are migrating and calving, the animals are often disoriented. There have been a number of instances in which moose actually charged automobiles.

As the numbers and range of moose increase, the number of collisions with cars has risen dramatically. In New Hampshire, accidents went from 49 in 1985 to 170 in 1989. Vermont had no car/moose collisions in 1980 but 41 in 1990. And in Maine, collisions went from 156 in 1980 to a whopping 500 in 1990. Yellow moose-crossing signs are now posted in areas moose are known to frequent.

The main opposition to restoring moose is most certainly the fear of vehicle collisions. The Draft Environmental Impact Statement issued by the Moose Restoration Project estimates one death every 2.6 years in the 20th year after the initial release of one hundred moose.

Any death on our highways is sobering, and one may or may not fully accept the EIS figures. But it is important to look at such figures in context. The DEC estimates that a driver in the 20th year would be ten times more likely to hit a bicyclist and twelve times more likely to hit a pedestrian than a moose.

In fact, there are many ways to go about saving lives on our highways. A decrease in the speed limit, increased law enforcement, greater funding for alcohol awareness programs and for driver education are all proven ways to save scores or even hundreds of lives a year on our highways. All it would take is the will to do so. But in fact, the speed limit in parts of New York State has actually been increased under the Pataki administration. Looked at from such a perspective, one might well question the seriousness of those who would single out the Moose Restoration Project as a threat to human lives. Such a position may be seen as little more than a cop-out to avoid serious efforts at making our highways safer. Indeed, if a small percentage of the private funds raised for the moose project were dedicated to driver education programs, the return of moose could actually *save* lives.

According to Hicks, surveys done in New Hampshire have shown that residents believe the return of moose is worth the risk. "Most people," Hicks says, "are simply thrilled to see a moose. Just the knowledge that they might see one can make a wilderness canoe trip into something quite special."

Despite all of this, the Moose Restoration Project was dropped for lack of public support, and the decision was made to allow moose to return at their own rate.

But given man's considerable contribution to the demise of moose in the Adirondacks, it would surely seem reasonable to give the animal a helping hand at a second chance. There have been other programs to reintroduce the lynx, the bald eagle, and the peregrine falcon. The return of the magnificent moose to its natural range must certainly rank at least as highly.

Bob Marshall Wilderness

While studying the map for the proposed Bob Marshall Great Wilderness, I realized that the area encompasses many of my favorite Adirondack locales. From the meandering Oswegatchie River in the Five Ponds Wilderness to the Bog River Flow to Lake Lila to Raquette Lake, the "Bob," at 408,000 acres, would be the biggest wilderness in the eastern United States north of the Everglades.

This was the dream of Bob Marshall, who originally identified the potential of the Cranberry Lake–Beaver River area in 1935. Conducting a national survey of all forest areas in the United States of at least 300,000 acres that had not been invaded by public transportation routes, Marshall hiked the region extensively in the 1920s, visiting nearly a hundred remote ponds.

Although Marshall died in his sleep at the age of thirty-eight, his dream of the "Bob" survived him and is today being encouraged by environmental groups. During his short but active life, Marshall served as chief of the Division of Recreation and Public Lands for the United States Forest Service, directed the forestry program of the Bureau of Indian Affairs, and founded the Wilderness Society along with Aldo Leopold and a few others.

But the Adirondack Park, where he had spent much of his youth at his family's camp on Lower Saranac Lake, became the foundation for Marshall's extraordinary vision for the future of our nation's wild lands. He was decades ahead of his time in this regard, arguing in 1935 in *The Living Wilderness* that "It is almost the rarest thing a human being can do today to escape the signs of mechanization. . . . The values which exist in such wilderness areas are very delicate. The mere knowledge that mechanization lies over the top of the hill is enough to destroy some of the finest inspirational values of the wilderness."

That these words could have been written over sixty years ago reminds us how much worse things have become. Their ring of truth has only grown with the passing decades. And yet, defying all the odds, the opportunity still exists today to preserve the Cranberry Lake–Beaver River country. Remarkably, it remains almost devoid of public roads.

If the Bob Marshall Great Wilderness becomes reality, it would encompass virtually all native Adirondack animals and ecosystems. It would include 441 lakes and ponds and 71 miles of waterways in the state's Wild, Scenic and Recreational Rivers System. Its 408,000 acres would give it status as a world-class nature reserve.

The state already owns 230,000 acres in the Bob. Private owners hold another 178,000 acres. The Adirondack Council has encouraged the state to promote good stewardship and to work to prevent subdivision and development by purchasing conservation easements from willing sellers.

The council has developed an extensive plan for the long-range implementation of the Bob Marshall Great Wilderness. Their recommendations are spelled out in the publication "2020 Vision—Fulfilling the Promise of the Adirondack Park."

Hopes for the Bob have been enhanced by the establishment in 1993 of an Environmental Protection Fund and by the bond act of 1996. For the first time in years, New York State has money to purchase lands and easements. However, as this book goes to press, the owners of Whitney Park have announced plans to subdivide and sell 15,000 acres, establishing forty lots for "great camps" and creating a hotel on Little Tupper Lake, the largest privately owned lake in the Adirondack Park. If this project is successful, the dream that Bob Marshall had so many years ago may be lost forever.

What's in a Name?

It is finally beginning to look like spring outside. The river behind my house grudgingly gives up its last icebergs. As I watch them float downstream by the hundreds, I feel not a smidgeon of regret.

The river is teeming with life. The great blue herons fly silently up and down its length on their endless quest for the perfect frog. Serenely, they glide in, land in the shallows behind my house, and commence the search. With stiff legs and jerking necks, they hunt with the single-mindedness of the wild creature. Once a frog is seized, they may spend as much as fifteen minutes gently washing it, or at least that is what it seems they are doing. Holding the hapless amphibian by a single leg, the heron swishes it back and forth, back and forth in the water. Finally, when some elemental moment has been reached, the frog is gone in an instant, down the gullet so quickly the watcher has missed the action.

The other birds common to this river are almost too numerous to name. Ducks and geese are everywhere, as are pheasant, kingfisher, owl, osprey, and even the lowly crow, which happens to be one of my favorites. The caw of the solitary crow is nearly as fine a sound to my ears as that of the loon.

Already this spring I have seen a pair of foxes, several deer, rabbits, weasels, porcupines, a badger, and a huge snapping turtle. I keep my eyes open for the elusive fisher, which I have seen here before. Otters have been scampering about, too, catching the small bass that my wife stocked the pond with several years ago. She looks out on them with a baleful eye. My advice to them is to be on their way.

The name of this river is Trout Brook, but it is no less a river for that slight of nomenclature. Behind my house it is forty feet wide and up to six feet deep. In fact, I have always taken a certain enjoyment from the term "brook," for it is a more colorful word than river in my mind.

Until now.

A month ago, the Solid Waste Disposal Authority announced that they had determined that this river was the best place in the county for a landfill. Now, I know the trash has to go somewhere. I didn't—and don't—like the idea of an incinerator, and a landfill (even with serious efforts at recycling) would seem to be a necessary evil. However, there is something alarmingly flawed with a site-selection process that chooses, for all practical purposes, to place a landfill on top of a beautiful river that teems with wildlife.

My first thought was that they couldn't really be serious. Rivers in their natural state are a rapidly vanishing phenomenon in this country. I was amused. A good joke, that. After all, people are always coming up with funny ways to get rid of our waste. "Shoot it into space," someone said to me recently, only half in jest. "Dump it down all those empty coal shafts in Pennsylvania," said another.

Pretty funny, I thought, the idea of putting it on top of Trout Brook. No need to worry about soil densities then. For that matter, why bother with any liners at all? This could be the perfect leachate system. Mother nature herself would dispose of—or is that disperse?—the stuff. There are many questions concerning landfill technology. There is no question, however, that sooner or later, they all leak.

Pretty funny.

Then they told me they were indeed serious. Such a nice, "central" location would make for economical hauling. Soil density looked good, too, and, of course, the area was appropriately inhabited by the poor, who could be counted on not to hire expensive lawyers to oppose the plan. All in all, a splendid location—simply no better place for a landfill in one of the largest counties east of the Mississippi. Nope. Trout Brook was "it." Just a brook, after all. And that was when I began to regret that name. The Grass, Oswegatchie, and Raquette were exempt. What did each of those waterways have that Trout Brook didn't? Only the word river after its name.

Trout River. Has a nice ring to it, don't you think?

Theater of the Absurd

To paraphrase former president Ronald Reagan: "There they go again." Members of the New York State Legislature have once again extended the legislative session because of an inability to get virtually anything done on time. Is this any way to run a state?

Our overpaid, part-time pols have moved on only a tiny fraction of the bills introduced during the session. Although the overwhelming majority of bills never go anywhere (most are simply introduced in order to get legislators' names in the paper), the inability to achieve significant accomplishments has, in 1993, reached new heights of incompetence.

In addition, by leaving everything until the last moment, legislators essentially bypass the democratic process. Since legislation comes out of committee following private deal-making behind closed doors, citizens are left with little or no time to react and comment on it. Indeed, legislators themselves have complained that they are asked by the leadership to vote on bills that they have not had time even to read, much less study. Bills as thick as telephone books regularly appear on lawmaker's desks only minutes before they must vote on the contents.

The flurry of last-minute negotiations over an Environmental Trust Fund is a case in point. New leaks emerge almost hourly— Senator Stafford refuses to allow any state land purchases in the Adirondacks, then he will allow two, then four, then the Whitney estate will be considered separately, and on and on. The public sits numb and dumb awaiting the pleasure of these powerbrokers who control our lives.

There is nothing new or even unusual (as legislative bodies go) about this process, but it stinks nonetheless. And it seems to be getting worse every year. The number of registered lobbyists working the state capital now tops eighteen hundred, up more than 100 percent since 1978. Lawmakers feel this pressure as they twist back and forth in the breeze of greenback-powered influence peddling. Clearly, it is easier for them to waffle and to give assurances to all sides on every issue and then leave town in a rush. By then, nearly everybody is unhappy, but at least the legislators don't have to be around to listen to the griping.

Many lawmakers play the game with unabashed zeal. The *New York Times* noted that by the end of the 1993 session, 128 of the legislature's 210 members had held fund-raisers in the capital—in a non-election year.

The name of this game is Keep the Lobbyists Happy and the Perks, Parties and Pork Flowing. The longer legislators can hold off on their decisions, the more money they can entice into their coffers.

Somebody needs to give this process a good going-over. The system is a mess. Everyone knows it. Nobody seems to be able to do anything about it. Although former governor Mario Cuomo and Assembly democrats have long supported proposals for public financing of legislative races, Senate Republicans refuse to go along.

With Governor Pataki now in command, it seems unlikely that campaign finance reform will soon top anyone's agenda.

Green Sevens and Other Theories

My four-year-old daughter announced the other day that seven and eight were her favorite numbers. When I asked why, she said it was because she liked their colors. You see, sevens are green and eights are purple.

There is no arguing with this sort of logic. I know. I've tried—with members of the so-called "Wise Use" movement, among others. Members of this group defend an individual's "right" to do whatever he chooses with his own land. You will have about as much luck trying to convince Wise Users that sevens aren't always green as you will have trying to explain to them that if everyone could do whatever they wished with their land, it just might cause problems—even in the la-la land of the Wise Users.

Particularly annoying to the Wise Users, who have lately been gaining a toehold in the Northeast, are the efforts of the Northern Forest Lands Council, an interstate study panel created by Congress, which has been attempting to find ways to protect this vast and complicated area from overdevelopment. The Northern Forest stretches from the western Adirondacks to the farthest seacoast of Maine. The council's report has been hailed as an important first step in the effort to take a regional approach to development problems. Although the council has no regulatory powers, and some have criticized this lack of teeth, just thinking about the Northern Forest as a unit is a sign of progress.

In a recent issue of *Wilderness*, Carl Reidel, director of the University of Vermont's environmental studies program at Montpelier, delineates his concern that population will spill into this region from urban

areas. "I'm very pessimistic," he writes. "When you think of the inex-
orable pressures of Boston, New York, or Montreal, if we don't do
some kind of careful work with green-lining or land-banking, I think
we're just going to see it fragmented. It could end up looking like all
the other parts of New England."

One of Reidel's greatest fears is the renewed interest in an "east-
west highway" that would run from Rutland, Vermont, straight into
the interior of Maine. I recently drove virtually this same route. The
most convenient way to do the drive now is on Route 2, a two-lane
highway that winds its way around mountains and rivers and passes
through innumerable small towns. It is frustratingly slow. But a new
highway would attract tens of thousands of people, many of whom
would begin to consider how nice it might be to own a camp or a
home on one of Maine's pristine lakes or rivers. That highway would
be the opening salvo in a development rush that might not end until,
as Reidel points out, the Northern Forest ends up "looking like all the
other parts of New England."

If we could all do precisely as we wished on our nation's remaining undeveloped and privately owned land, I suspect even the Wise
Users might eventually catch on to the horror they are promoting.

Maybe. But first, someone needs to take the blinders off these
people. The truth is, Wise Users are no different from other land-
owners. They preen about their right to do whatever they want on
their land, but like the rest of us, they head to the nearest lawyer if a
stinky wood pulp factory moves in upwind or if a neighbor decides
to put his septic tank ten feet from their well or if a hunter next door
takes to shooting at deer that are standing in their front yards.

Neighbors sometimes do stupid things. They can't always be
trusted. It's why we have laws. It's why we can't always do whatever
we want on our own land. In theory, a man's home is his castle. But
listen, it's only a theory.

My daughter thinks sevens can only be green. But that's only a
theory too.

More Money than Common Sense

A dispute over water ownership in the town of Callicoon, New York, struck a familiar chord with me when I read about it. It seems that one Andrew J. Krieger bought land there in the late 1980s and proceeded to develop a business selling the area's crystal-pure aquifer waters to the Great Bear Spring Company, a subsidiary of Perrier.

Mr. Krieger's neighbors are crying foul, saying his water farm has spoiled the environment, dried up nearby trout streams and caused wildlife to disappear. This is no small concern as the area's economy depends on the attraction of tourists to trout streams that have become known throughout the world. One local resident wrote to the town questioning Krieger's ownership of the water: "Can anyone truly be given permission to sell ground or surface water simply because they flow through that person's property? . . . Water can no longer be considered an infinite resource."

Here is where the dispute rang a bell with me, for it sounded so much like the arguments made by private game clubs and other landholders who have long kept boating recreationists off Adirondack rivers.

Simply by virtue of the fact that a river flows through their land, these property owners have declared the rivers closed to all citizens for boating purposes—this in a state park long dedicated to "the free use of all the people" and in support of which all New Yorkers pay taxes. If an individual happens to own half an acre on both sides of a rapids that requires a ten-foot carry, miles of navigable waterway are effectively shut down to recreation in perpetuity.

There is a faction in this country that has long taken to the idea that property ownership is a nearly divine right. If they have the piece of paper that says they own the land, then they by God OWN IT and can do anything they want with it.

Of course, they are wrong right off the bat. There are myriad laws controlling what one can do on one's own land. You can't stand on your own ground and shoot someone who happens on it innocently. Nor can you fire at a plane that flies over it. You can't dump toxic waste on it, can't decide to hold a Woodstock or blast with dynamite without special permit, you can't import exotic fish that will destroy existing species, can't open a nudist colony, and can't even burn down your own home. You can't shoot animals that come on it out of season, you can't booby-trap the place, you can't print your own money on it, and you can't declare yourself a separate country and refuse to pay your taxes.

Nope. Just can't do any of those things. Imagine—pesky old laws.

The world is growing too small to allow this sort of frontier attitude any longer. There are simply too many of us now and we are everywhere from the mountains of Tierra Del Fuego to the Arctic tundra. Almost anything anyone does anywhere now affects other people. The old saying, "Your right to swing your fist ends where my nose begins" has never been more accurate.

Mr. Krieger's right to bottle water on his land ends when he causes the rivers to run dry and the animals to disappear. The only problem in today's litigious society is proving beyond a reasonable doubt the true source of the trouble. Mr. Krieger claims that a general drought in the region is the real cause of the stated environmental problems. Given the amount of money involved, he appears to be willing to spend quite a bit of it on lawyers.

Similarly, although the Department of Environmental Conservation finally took a reasonable attitude and refused to prosecute boaters passing through private land in the Adirondacks, at least one large hunting club has gone to court over the matter. There the issue has languished for years.

Some people have more money than common sense.

They Will Come

For years, a small but very vocal group of Adirondack residents has raised an unholy ruckus over the "outrageous" restrictions on development within the park. Led by developers and real estate and banking interests, there has been a full-court effort to convince the public that any sort of restriction whatsoever will lead to economic disaster.

As is often the case, to dig beneath the surface of what doomsayers espouse is to uncover a mine of greed and self-interest. The only economic disaster looming anywhere will likely be to a few totally uncontrolled and uncontrollable contractors and loan officers. Most people, even in the Adirondack Park, know this. But they are outspent by the moneyed interests.

Now we have some new evidence to suggest that those sky-is-falling forecasters are all hot air. In Oregon, doomsayers predicted that the restrictions placed on logging in 1991 to protect the northern spotted owl would lead to massive layoffs, foreclosures, crippling recession, and the creation of ghost towns.

Surprise. Three years later, unemployment is the lowest in a generation at 5 percent. The *New York Times* reports that Oregon lost fifteen thousand jobs in the last five years in forest product industries. But it gained twenty thousand jobs in high technology. By the end of next year, high technology will surpass timber as the leading source of jobs in the state. In the last year, one hundred thousand jobs have been added to Oregon's economy—the exact number the timber industry said would be lost as a result of the restrictions. No county in Oregon has an unemployment rate higher than 7.8 percent. In some rural counties, the rate is 2 percent, four points under the national rate.

How did all this happen? For one thing, mills found they could just as easily replace old-growth timber with farm-grown wood products. And many of those timber workers who did lose their jobs got job-training assistance and are now employed in other areas. Very few have had to rely upon low-paying, burger-flipping jobs. Many declare that the forced changes have opened up new opportunities and personal growth.

Again, from The *New York Times:* Dr. Ed Whitelaw, professor of economics at the University of Oregon, says: "These 100,000-job-loss figures were just fallacious; they came out of a political agenda. Yet when I would say this, I was dismissed as an Earth-Firster or something." And Bill Morrisette, mayor of Springfield, Oregon, put the obvious truth even more clearly: "Owls versus jobs was just plain false. What we've got here is quality of life. And as long as we don't screw that up, we'll always be able to attract people and business."

Michael Burrill, owner of a timber mill in Medford, Oregon, had declared that saving the spotted owl would create Appalachia in the Northwest. Listen to what he says now: "We've had an awful lot of new industry, and that's surprised me. . . . Turns out there's a hell of a lot going on."

The greatest resource we have in the Adirondacks is our pristine environment. That and a little ingenuity can more than make up for the necessary changes and controls needed to protect this great wilderness. "Quality of life." That is what attracts people to the beautiful scenery of the Northwest. And it is what attracts them to our own Adirondacks.

The doomsayers, the developers and bankers and real estate agents are dead wrong when they say restrictions are hurting the local economy. The real truth?

If you don't build on it—they will come.

Greedlock in the Florida Keys

Greed and stupidity are killing the Florida Keys, writes Philip Caputo in a *New York Times* magazine article. "Once a place like no other, [the Keys] had become like any other place in America; noisy, congested, ugly."

The decay of the Keys went into fast gear with the completion of a multimillion-dollar reconstruction of the lone highway in 1983. As a result, the jeweled chain of reefs that spin out of the bottom of Florida like the tail of a comet has been transformed—one fears forever.

I can remember the Keys in a different time. I visited them in 1970 while on spring break from school. They were much as Caputo described them back then: quiet, with a laid-back, small-town atmosphere. The hundred-mile drive to Key West seemed to take forever on the narrow highway where opportunities to pass slow-moving vehicles were almost nonexistent. That slow road, it now appears, was all that was protecting the Keys from modern tourism.

Although there was certainly development in 1970, it was of the small, locally owned variety. Weathered old motels, bars, and marinas were scattered here and there, but I don't recall being offended by their presence. My friend and I, recently steeped in Hemingway lore, were ripe for adventure, our first choice being to climb Mt. Kilimanjaro in Africa. But our finances were not up to that. Key West seemed just the thing.

The town was quiet and uncrowded even at the height of the tourist season. We wandered about making the obligatory visits to Sloppy Joe's and Hemingway's home. I remember being fascinated by Sloppy Joe's, a huge, square sort of thing in the center of town with enormous doors open to the street. Inside, the walls were lined with Hemingway memorabilia and stuffed fish. The large, slow-moving ceiling fans made me feel as though I'd arrived in Casablanca or Havana. To top it off, I was stunned to discover that the men's room had a coin-operated condom dispenser. Talk about avant-garde! Years later, I was to learn that in all likelihood, that bar had not really been the one where Hemingway went after all.

The only overcrowding we experienced came when we visited the Hemingway home. Not from the tourists. In fact, we very nearly had the place to ourselves. The overcrowding was from the cats. Before he died, Hemingway arranged for his many cats and their descendants to have the run of the place. They did. Our guide informed us that there were something on the order of forty or fifty cats in residence at the time. They lounged around the enormous pool like so many retired fat cats from Miami Beach.

But that Key West is gone. Today, the Keys are wall-to-wall condos, fast-food franchises, and chain motels. Acres of mangrove and dogwood, in a place that has no acres to spare, have been bulldozed into oblivion, and it is a rare opportunity indeed to be able to see the ocean without a neon sign in front of it. The very reefs are dying as the coral is killed off by sewage and the other effluents of sardine-packaged man.

I doubt very much that I will ever bother to go back to Key West. I want to keep those memories intact. But as I look in my own backyard and see the same sorts of things going on in the Adirondacks, I want to cry out. For it all went away so very quickly in the Keys—a decade was long enough.

Some say it can't happen in the Adirondacks. But that is exactly what they said about the Keys.

Our Adirondack Niche

Pressures on the National Park system have been growing by leaps and bounds. Whenever I hear about these problems, I can only feel thankful for our own Adirondack Park. Although the Adirondacks have an estimated nine million annual visitors, the park is so vast that one rarely experiences overcrowding if the more obvious resort centers are avoided.

By way of contrast, Yellowstone has been described as an urban tourist ghetto with garbage, noise, crime, and traffic all rampant. Yosemite recently had over three million visitors in its much smaller area. And all of the parks are being degraded by the addition of unnecessary conveniences and accommodations for the tourist. Yosemite's wilderness now boasts restaurants, bars, hotels, an ice skating rink, stables, and shopping malls. This is wilderness? A Central Park would be more like it.

There has been much discussion about the concessionaires, the private companies that run the park facilities. Although they conduct over half a billion dollars worth of business every year, the government receives only $12.5 million in fees from them. The presence of these virtual corporations within the parks raises serious questions concerning the way our park system is organized.

During the eight years of the Reagan presidency, park programs that focused on the environment were cut in half. Only about 1 percent of all park funding now goes for such research. The parks postponed maintenance over the past decade to such an extent that they now face a two-billion-dollar backlog of repairs. There is little money available in these times of budget cuts and deficits to address the problems.

From time to time, the idea has been raised of making the Adirondacks into a National Park. Laurence S. Rockefeller made such a proposal in 1967, but he fortunately met with almost universal resistance to the plan. Indeed, such an idea should horrify all New Yorkers. The redesignation would certainly mean many, many more visitors to the Adirondacks. And it is highly unlikely that the Adirondack Park's unusual mixture of public and private lands would make for a feasible National Park venture. Indeed, it might set a bad precedent for the other parks. A developer might point to the Adirondacks and say: "See. What's so bad about a little private ownership within a National Park?"

In addition, placing the park under the aegis of federal control, while perhaps meaning some additional funding, would almost surely lead to many of the problems now facing the other parks. The fifty National Parks and 307 monuments and cultural and historical sites now within the park system are already overburdening a Park Service that seems to be first on every politician's list at budget-cutting time.

This may be something of a selfish position for a New Yorker to take. Perhaps if more reserves like the Adirondacks were added to the national system, it would relieve some of the pressure on the existing parks. Perhaps. More likely, it seems to me, is that we would simply sacrifice one more glorious piece of our country to the tourist hordes. More than 250 million visits a year are now paid to the parks, a number expected to double within twenty years. I have often been surprised—and pleasantly so—when I talk about the Adirondacks with people from other states. Few have any idea what we have here. Once designated a National Park, that anonymity would disappear.

Certainly, the Adirondacks are not without their own considerable problems from overdevelopment and the loss of scenic vistas to pollution and acid rain. Struggles over the past few years to come to some kind of consensus as to the proper mix of public and private land use within the park illustrate the difficulties facing New Yorkers. But it stretches credulity to believe that becoming part of the National Park system would solve any of these issues.

One of the areas of deep concern for all of the parks, including the Adirondacks, is that of encroachment. Our parks no longer have viable boundaries to such national and global problems as acid rain and air pollution. The list of dangers to the parks is long and complex—logging along park lines has destroyed wildlife refuges at Olympic National Park in Washington, domestic sheep in Utah have wiped out herds of Canyonland's big horn sheep with disease, Las Vegas threatens to drain Death Valley National Monument of its limited springs, and residential development is creeping right up to park borders everywhere. Many studies have declared that our parks can not survive as wilderness islands in a sea of urbanity.

The National Park service celebrated its seventy-fifth birthday in 1991. It has been a glorious experiment, one of our nation's greatest contributions to humanity. It remains to be seen, however, if we will have the conviction and strength of purpose to tackle its many problems before it is too late.

Perspectives

All the thoughts of a turtle are turtle.

—RALPH WALDO EMERSON

Sounds of Silence

Scientists the world over tell us that the woods are growing quieter. Species depletion, they call it. The songbirds are disappearing. The frogs are dying off. Ducks and geese find fewer and fewer undrained wetlands to land upon.

I spend a fair amount of time in the woods, but I'm not sure I can lend much to this discussion from a personal viewpoint. My hearing seems to be dying off at its own steady rate as I grow older. I am no longer certain if the lack of sound in the woods is from fewer hermit thrushes and white-throated sparrows or merely from fewer hearing receptors within my own auricular canal.

I read not long ago that the annual bird count by the Audubon Society was having difficulty getting accurate numbers for certain highly pitched species because many of the group's members were getting on in years and could no longer hear the birds. The society was considering a recommendation that the counts be divided up, with younger members listening for the more highly pitched species. But I don't believe that recommendation was adopted. Someone apparently suggested that it might put pressure on older birders to fake their counts in order to be allowed to go on doing this good work they had enjoyed for so long. An unlikely scenario, in my opinion. The birders I have known would never do such a thing. They consider their annual count a sacred trust.

But of course the losses are real.

The Costa Rican golden toad is gone. The Peruvian variegated toad is gone. The Gambian reed frog is gone. From Cameroon to Borneo, from the Andes to the Alps, frogs, toads, and salamanders are disappearing as though wiped from the slate of life by a magic wand.

No one knows why this is happening, although possible explanations abound—acid rain, ozone depletion, loss of habitat, etc. More likely, it is the effect of something we have yet to discover. We have introduced so many hundreds of thousands of chemicals into this experimental crucible we call earth that almost anything is possible.

Perhaps these species of frogs and toads are too exotic for their loss to make much impression on our lives. But they are almost certainly a harbinger. Just suppose when next you go canoeing down that marvelous chain of lakes comprising the St. Regis Canoe area, that you might never again see another mallard or whitetail or, God forbid, a loon.

Even if I should go stone deaf, I would still hear the loons in my mind—if they still existed. But if they were gone, I think my overwhelming sense of loss would keep me from calling forth that haunting cry.

Canoeing is, in essence, the art of listening. It is perhaps the most perfectly silent mode of travel ever devised—a characteristic understood and utilized fully by the aboriginal hunter. If the forest truly is growing quieter, then paddlers (at least the young ones or those with good hearing aids) ought to be the first to know.

There simply is no better way to approach wildlife closely before they are aware you are there. I've spent an entire afternoon lazily chasing a heron or a pair of ducks down miles of winding river. Every time I round a bend and surprise them yet again, they honk or quack in alarm as though I were some apparition never before seen rather than just the same old boat disturbing their routine for the tenth time.

On the water is also the only time when I hear the weather—really hear it. I listen to every breath of change in the wind from the light rustle of dry fall leaves to the roar of a heavy gale through a tall stand of white pine. On a still and heavily overcast afternoon, I hear the first drops of a rainfall, and sometimes I think I hear the sunlight breaking through the clouds—it can break those clouds very noisily when it wants to.

The forest has its own music, and I should miss it very much if the frogs and the toads or indeed any of its instruments were to disappear.

Answering Essential Questions

Paddling sports have become more and more popular in recent years. The small boat enthusiast may choose anything from sailing on the open ocean to puttering in and out of tiny, winding streams and across spring flood-swollen fields. There is something exhilarating about floating soundlessly through a farmer's fields, visiting in an entirely new way what may be familiar ground.

The true canoeist, however, shuns large lakes or open ocean for the quiet, meandering stream. For this, the canoe was invented, many times in many parts of the world, for ease of travel, light weight, flexibility of movement, and the quiet required by the aboriginal hunter. Here, every twist and turn offers a completely new vista, a sunset is seen from a hundred different angles, and the same towering white pine may be viewed against a dozen varying backdrops.

One of the more troubling aspects of modern society is its endless choices. Canoeing simplifies even as it amplifies the human experience.

At home, choices for entertainment seem to abound. Shall we watch TV, listen to radio, or read a book? If TV, which of seventy channels shall it be? If radio, do we choose classical, jazz, news, sports, or entertainment of a hundred different varieties? Books? Will we choose to improve ourselves by plowing through the classics, inform ourselves by reading a magazine, or entertain ourselves with a mystery?

Out on the river, all the options become marvelously concentrated. No TV and no radio (the occasional boom-boxer aside—no nature lovers these). What to read? One book at most can be taken when weight is a consideration. Take something you always meant to read, and I guarantee you will find yourself finally plowing through it no matter what the topic.

Choices.

What to eat? At home, the refrigerator contains enough material to construct a score of different meals. Better yet, how about going out to that special French restaurant, order home delivery of a pizza, or just head for the corner deli?

On the river, dining is simplicity itself. All choices of food have been made days, if not weeks, in the past. And the wonder of it—every bite tastes like nectar when eaten under a hanging outcrop as the rain falls, your body aching from the last carry, or when taken at dusk as you sit looking out over a mirrored lake, the loons calling, the sun setting, your camp awaiting the night behind you.

Choices.

Companionship at home means deciding among dozens of friends whom one will spend the evening or weekend with. Do we go with the relatives not seen for a while? Do we really want to see the Cousteaus this evening with that obnoxious three-year-old that they take everywhere with them? Or spend the evening with Jack the Jock who will regale us with tales of his latest triathlon in Kuala Lumpur?

On the river, my choice of friend and companion has been made long ago, after years of testing and finding his company the most compatible of any in the woods. We are alone together, and though he may occasionally test my temper by paddling in that contrary fashion, I know him well. Of necessity, we have talked of everything from the mundane chores of camplife to the great philosophical questions of our age as we float downstream. I seem to know when he wants to talk; he seems to intuit when I want nothing more than to listen to the wind. Sharing the same experience, we become closer and know each other better than any of our city-bound acquaintances.

Canoeing is simplification. When to go to bed? Why, when you are tired of course or when your oil lamp runs low. When to break camp in the morning? After chores certainly, followed by a hearty breakfast, that is when the water beckons. When to stop for the day? When that perfect campsite appears—even if it's only midday. What to wear? Whatever the weather dictates.

Samuel Johnson wrote: "When a man is tired of London, he is tired of life." I say, when a man is tired of London, he should head for the out-of-doors, a quiet river, a good friend, and a trusty canoe, and he will renew himself as no city has or ever could renew a man.

Taking a Stern Position

One ongoing debate I have with my primary canoeing partner, Jim, concerns the relative merits and demerits of the bow versus stern positions. Raise the issue among paddlers, and particularly paddlers who often go on lengthy wilderness trips, and you will get as many opinions as there are canoes on the lake.

Jim and I have been canoeing together for about twenty years. When we first started out, we tended not to talk much about where we preferred to sit. Whoever was standing next to the stern after all the gear was loaded became the stern man, simple as that. But then an incident occurred which more or less fixed our positions forever.

I had begun to reside more often in the stern (Jim tends to pack and organize meticulously and had developed a back support that only fit the bow seat). Thus, by the time we had canoed together for four or five years, this setup had become the norm. Then one day I happened to get into the bow after perhaps two full years of not sitting there. I fell in love with the position.

The first thing I noticed was that sitting in the bow was a lot like being in the nose cone of a glider, something I'd once had the opportunity to do. There you were, right up front with absolutely nothing between you and the rest of the world. I realized that for those past two years, I had spent more of my time gazing at Jim's back and at the mound of our gear than I had at my surroundings. But this! This was like being in front of a panoramic motion picture of the out-of-doors. Suddenly, it was possible to lose myself completely in the setting. I was astounded to discover how much the presence of the rest of the canoe and all of its manmade contraptions (including the man) managed to intrude on my emotions. Simply put, the stern man finds the commercial world too much with him. All day long, the view is of the L. L. Bean boots lying on top of the duffle, of the Coleman lantern, and of the garishly colored watertight bags. And whenever Jim lights up his pipe, which he is wont to do periodically, the smoke invariably drifts back into my face. It is very hard to be a philosopher or a dreamer in the stern.

With my discovery, I now wanted to be in the bow all the time. For Jim's part, he discovered a new passion for steering. The power of being in control, of adjusting the course with the merest flick of the wrist, was intoxicating. We were both happy in our newfound joys.

Then we paddled down Moosehead Rapids on the Raquette River.

Moosehead Rapids is not particularly arduous. Primarily Class III rapids, its main difficulty lies in its continuous nature. There are only a few spots to rest for well over a mile. We negotiated about half of the rapids without incident. I was settling into the comfortable use of the drawstroke, used by the bowman to change course quickly when a last minute rock is detected.

We had entered a stretch with a long straightaway. At the end of this straightaway was a single boulder in the exact middle of the river. I saw this rock while we were still about a hundred yards from it. It was quite large and I accepted its presence as simply part of the scenery. Such a big boulder. Jim certainly had seen it.

Except.

Except we made our way down that straightaway in an almost perfectly straight line. Jim paddled steadily, proud of his newfound ability to keep us on an even keel. For my part, I never imagined for an instant that Jim could not see that boulder.

Jim could not see that boulder.

It was situated precisely in front of me, and Jim's view of it was completely blocked by my own body. We approached at a fairly good clip as the current maintained its force. I am a trusting soul. I never doubted Jim's ability to steer us around the obstacle. All that was needed was a slight course correction—one that could be made even at the last moment.

The boulder was shaped almost like the blade of a plow with the shallow end facing us and the slant running away to a height of several feet down river.

With perfect aplomb, Jim steered us directly onto the plow. Our craft rose up out of the water, went halfway up the rock and neatly turned us over into the cold water. I do not believe I realized what would happen until we were just two or three feet from the rock. The last thing I recall saying was: "You do see that rock, don't you?"

The incident at Moosehead Rapids became a defining moment in our canoeing lives. I returned to the stern; Jim took his place at the bow, and we have never altered again. Today, whenever the notion strikes Jim to take a turn in the stern, I shout, "Remember Moosehead!"

And we paddle on.

Luxury Canoes

If you're looking for something new to invest in, don't call Louis Reukeyser; I can advise you. The best place for your money in the nineties is canoes. I'm not talking about collectors' items, although early Rushtons and Old Towns have certainly appreciated at astounding rates.

No. What I'm talking about are brand new, state-of-the-art, fresh-from-the-factory canoes and kayaks. These will soon be the status symbols of the late 20th century—the kreugerrands and diamonds of the jet investment set.

The luxury yacht business is dead. The combination of the recession and a new 10 percent federal luxury tax on any boat priced above a nontaxable floor of $100,000 has devastated boatworks across the nation. And it hasn't helped individuals like Donald Trump much either. His initial $100,000,000 asking price for the *Trump Princess* has gone begging. What's a fellow to do?

Maybe you think the rich are different from you and me. After all, what are a few more tax dollars to them? But consider. The luxury tax on a $200,000 boat would be $10,000. Connecticut's 8 percent sales tax would add another $16,000. That's $26,000 in taxes. If you are considering something a little more expensive, say in the half-million-dollar range, you can add a tidy $80,000 to the cost.

Like the man said, "A billion here, a billion there, and pretty soon you're talking real money."

Yes, for once, the rich are really taking it on the chin. The luxury tax also applies to new cars that cost more than $30,000, airplanes over $250,000, and furs and jewelry over $10,000. Sales of these commodities are slumping. But before you start passing the hat for The Donald, remember this—the rich have powerful friends. Some members of Congress are already seeking repeal of the luxury tax. If only they could act on an education bill with such speedy concern for their constituents.

Back to our canoe investment. Clearly, there is going to be a lot more money going into canoes with all those luxury yacht funds freed up by panicky millionaires. Quick as you can say Michael Jackson, the upper crust's accountants will be advising them to buy Kyll Spectrum 2.25s, Topo Duo K2s, K-1 W Hawk Club Racers, and Gyra-Max C-1s. I am not making the names of these boats up.

The need to top your neighbor's luxury canoe will take on new meaning. Before you know it, Madonna will be floating past you in her new six-portal baidarka with attendant butlers, masseuse, French chef, and full wet bar. Bodyguards will have to make do in support flotillas of Rob Roys.

The urge to add a certain cachet, a *je ne sais quois* to the canoe of your choice will be uppermost in every investment banker's mind. Kayaks will come with built-in personal computers, remote sensor tracking, and satellite guidance systems. Kevlar and fiberglass will be passé, replaced by Russian sable and Gore-Tex, custom-fitted by tailors from Saville Row. Paint jobs? Now to be commissioned by the Jackson Pollacks and Andy Warhols of the new canoe painters' guild.

And then—stretch canoes.

An idea whose time has clearly come, they will replace the limos that are already under attack by the luxury tax. There will be no limit to the lengths Ivana might go to top her ex. She may not have gotten half the five billion, but her 250-foot stretch canoe will dwarf the *Trump Princess.*

Remember—you heard it here first. Get your savings into canoes. Fast.

Perceptions

I slipped out for some cross-country skiing the other day. It was a sunny and crisp afternoon and there were plenty of people on the trail. At one point, I passed a couple who had left the main path and were some forty or fifty feet off in the brush. They had binoculars with them and were staring raptly up into the trees. Although I looked all about, I couldn't see what it was they were staring at. Not wanting to disturb them, I continued on my way as silently as possible.

Just a few moments later, I had to move quickly out of the track to allow what was obviously a practicing racer to stroke by. He was moving at approximately three times my normal pace and paid no attention whatsoever to me as I slowly sank into three feet of soft snow in his wake. He was also completely wired for sound.

To each his own. But I could not help reflecting on the differences between the racer and the bird watchers. Their perceptions of this place that they were both so obviously enjoying must have been worlds apart. The couple with the binoculars were clearly much more tuned to their surroundings, willing to stop and look and listen. The racer had only one thing on his mind—speed, and perhaps Gloria Estefan or whatever group he was listening to on the headphones.

I don't want to suggest, really, that the racer was doing anything intrinsically wrong. He was enjoying himself, getting exercise, was probably well engaged in his own world, perhaps thinking great thoughts for all I knew. It's a well-known fact that today's young people can exercise, carry on a telephone conversation, watch TV, and study for an exam in quantum mechanics all at the same time.

But what I might suggest they can't do while doing all these other things, is develop a real love and understanding of the natural world around them. If there was a bird in a tree anywhere near this fellow, he wouldn't have heard it over the blast of "music" in his ears. And any wildlife along his route would have been scared away by the sound of his noisily slapping skis as he strove for ever greater speed.

People are different and that's a fact. Just think of all the ways they enjoy the same beautiful piece of the outdoors—skiers, snow-mobilers, bird watchers, nature photographers, campers, canoeists, speedboat racers, hang-gliders, dirt-bikers, ATV'ers, snowshoers, mountain climbers, kayakers—all are getting something deeply personal and satisfying from the same bit of landscape.

But I would also argue that not all are equally aware of their surroundings, of the many other living things that want to share the place with them, of the varied stresses that the forest or stream may be undergoing, of the long-term impact of the presence of lots of people or even of plans for development that may be taking place on a drawing board somewhere.

My only point is that if you enjoy the out-of-doors for whatever activity, take a moment to stop what you are doing and simply "feel" the place. Stop, look, listen, and "feel."

Usually, that's all that it really takes.

Hatchet Job

Paddlers love to argue over equipment. There is good reason for this, because every bit of one's gear has to be hauled across the various carries. As a result, weight has become the defining element in these arguments, and every equipment manufacturer has put significant R & D into paring down the weight.

But there is one useful piece of equipment that I have yet to see conveniently reduced from its basic elements, and that is the hatchet. Yes, it is possible to buy a folding hatchet, but these are not terribly efficient, in my opinion. For in hatchets, sturdiness and balance are all.

This may come as a surprise to many of you. All the thing is good for, I hear you say, is splitting wood. Any hatchet can do that job reasonably well. Wrong! Wrong! Wrong!

The primary woodland function of the hatchet is its ability to be thrown. Anyone who has been ten years old knows this. Years ago, when I first began paddling, my partner and I discussed this issue at some length.

In those days, we debated the merits of equipment endlessly. This was largely the result of having become the butts of family jokes about our supply techniques. These (childish) jokes would run along the lines of "I see you've got enough chips and beer to last till Armageddon" or "Have you considered pulling a pack canoe behind you for the extra food?" All true paddlers will understand the hurt of such comments.

As I sometimes use a canoe called the Pack, made by Old Town, this last joke struck to the quick. To be honest, we did take a lot of food along on our early outings, but we were still learning in those days. Believe me, the last thing you want to be is up the Oswegatchie without your Oreos.

In fact, the truth can now be revealed that Jim and I pioneered many early camping innovations, from the use of the pack canoe to the voyageur carbo-up method of building energy reserves. For this purpose, we developed a recipe for oatcakes that called for four table-spoons of Crisco per oatcake. The voyageurs were themselves re-nowned for their culinary inventiveness, constructing appetizing meals of rotting salt pork and birch bark tea. This was known as "living off the land" and was widely respected among outdoorsmen of the Fess Parker School.

But getting back to that hatchet. I was an early graduate of the Fess Parker School, having learned at the age of eight how to split a shingle nailed to the trunk of a tree by throwing a hatchet at it. It took me the better part of a year, six broken hatchets, and a severely trau-matized maple tree to learn this valuable outdoor skill. But it was a small price to pay for the pleasure attained when Lisa Stanton hap-pened to drop by my house one afternoon on her way home from school. I proceeded to tell her that I could split a shingle with my hatchet at ten paces. She gave me that "I wouldn't believe anything a boy of ten told me if he swore it on a stack of Davy Crockett comic books" look.

So naturally, I pulled out my hatchet, told Lisa to stand back out of harm's way, and threw it neatly through the center of the afore-mentioned shingle. Pieces of shingle went flying in all directions and the hatchet stuck firmly in the (by now) nearly barkless maple tree.

Awe is the only word to describe the look on Lisa's face. I saun-tered over and retrieved my hatchet with a manly tug, slid it back into my belt loop, and casually looked over my shoulder to see if there were any hostiles approaching.

So now I should think you more clearly understand the impor-tance of that lowly piece of equipment to the average outdoorsman. I never go on a camping trip without it.

And by the way, I never threw that hatchet again. Why tempt the fates?

The Dwindling Earth

The amount of wilderness left untouched by man grows smaller with each passing year. In truth, it can be argued that there is none at all when one considers that even the remotest parts of the globe are now affected by acid rain, global warming, ozone depletion, and so forth. Bill McKibben argues as much in his book *The End of Nature*.

It disturbs me that this dwindling of the earth's natural state doesn't seem to bother a lot of people. How is it that they are unable to make the relatively small leap of understanding necessary to see that it is their own survival that is at stake? The answer, I fear, lies in the very way we live and interact with the world today. For most of us are no longer a part of nature. We have become separate and apart.

The Census Bureau reports that 25 percent of Americans now live in cities and another 50 percent in their surrounding suburbs. No more than one person in four lives in a rural environment. Our cities spew out into the surrounding farmland, expanding fiercely in all directions. The northeastern seaboard from Maine all the way to the Chesapeake Bay is essentially one vast, sprawling city. Where the first explorers once saw nothing but towering forests of pine and spruce, they would now see little but concrete, condominiums, communication wires, and cars. A new race has evolved upon the earth—suburban man.

Until 1960, New York was one of the two most urban states in the nation. Today it is only in 10th place. The greatest urbanization has occurred in California, which now boasts a population that is, incredibly, 93 percent urban. The most rural state in the nation is tiny Vermont, where a respectable 68 percent still have managed to avoid the city.

What does it mean? For one thing, it means that most people have little understanding of nature because their only contact with it comes in the form of city parks or zoos. That's being generous. In fact, the majority probably get no closer to nature than the flower pot on the windowsill or the dirt ball field down the block where the kids go to play baseball.

Some cities have literally turned their backs on the out-of-doors by building vast underground malls with connecting corridors. Not surprisingly, the greatest of these occur in the north where the weather can occasionally be troublesome. Toronto has created an entire underground city. Her people needn't bother coming to the surface all winter long if they are so inclined. I suspect some of these Morlocks don't come out even in the summer.

There must be a real sense of puzzlement in such people when they hear others raising a fuss about strange species dying out in the jungles of Brazil or about forests perishing in Germany or about vast dead areas in our oceans. Where's the relevance to their lives? At most, it means the local fish market hasn't any orange roughy today or that there seem to be fewer songbirds visiting the bird feeder.

With three out of four Americans living so utterly out of contact with the natural world, it becomes a little easier to understand their lack of interest in "the end of nature." Our society is essentially run by such people—bureaucrats, businessmen, lawyers, and politicians.

Especially politicians.

Not only do they spend all their time in cities, but you can be sure that they are aware of the fact that three out of four of their constituents live there too—in splendid isolation from nature.

But like it or not, we are all tied to the land—even if most of us never walk in a forest, feel a sea breeze, or tramp up a mountain. Whether we live in a cabin in the outback or a penthouse on Park Avenue, "the end of nature" will knock on all of our doors.

Wind

While cross-country skiing, I pause for a moment on the trail to stare up at a tall stand of ramrod-straight red pines. They are about a foot in diameter and rise to a height of some sixty feet or more. As I look at them, a brisk breeze suddenly comes up and just as quickly dies away, its approach and departure reminiscent of the Doppler sound effect of a passing freight train. The tops of the trees scribe circles in the sky and their trunks creak in protest. The entire episode lasts only a few seconds but serves to remind me yet again how much pleasure I take from the wind.

In fact, I have never known anyone to truly enjoy the out-of-doors and not also love the wind.

John Muir reveled in it in his own inimitable way—from atop a one-hundred-foot Douglas fir, whipping back and forth in gale force winds.

Thoreau wrote, "These March winds, which make the woods roar and fill the world with life and bustle, appear to wake up the trees out of their winter sleep and excite the sap to flow."

And Shelley called the west wind:

> Wild Spirit, which art moving everywhere;
> Destroyer and preserver
> . . . .
> tameless, and swift, and proud.

Wind derives its character from the landscape it crosses. No squall stirring whitecaps in midocean can truly be the same as the fresh breeze that permeates a forest, creating its own distinctive roar.

Nor can a gust gently rustling the leaves of fall be mistaken for the zephyr that silently turns a field of wheat from auburn to silver and back again. "Winds," Muir wrote, "are advertisements of all they touch."

If I were free to live in any place, I would choose one subject to the most awesome and continuous of winds. Perhaps the top of Mt. Washington would serve, that home to two hundred mile-per-hour record-setters. Or better—a stone tower overlooking the furthest outposts of Scotland.

My soundest slumbers come to the background music of a howling nor'easter. Such a storm produces a white noise unlike any other, one that soothes the soul yet brings intimations of an earlier time—a wilder time when men huddled in caves or under prairie skies and listened to storms embodied by their fears with demons and gods.

I feel the spell of human history in every windstorm—the chill winds that swept the Vikings west to Greenland, the hot khamsin breezes that drove Gordon's boats up the Nile to Khartoum, and the monsoons that wiped out whole villages in Asia. I feel it in the squalls, gales, and storms that beset poor sailors and tried their skills in every age—and in the typhoons, hurricanes, and tempests that proved too much for them and sent them down to where the wind never blows.

The simoom, harmattan, scirroco, levanter, tramontane, chinook, mistral, bise, and foehn—winds from every corner of the globe. There is a sense of timelessness to these aerodynamics. The winds wear down the landscape the way time wears down our lives. In the end, the passage of time returns us all to the earth in the same way that the wind eventually returns the mountain to the sea.

It is good to acknowledge the wind. In the words of the painter Nelson Augustus Moore: "How few [ever] notice the sky? Who saw the dance of the dead clouds last night, when the sun had left them, and they were driven before the blast like withered leaves?"

The wind is nature's paintbrush, the world her canvas.

The Root Hole

Each March, my thoughts turn to the Oswegatchie highlands. After months of ice and snow, I begin to itch for the sight of open water. The river trip from Inlet to High Falls and beyond is widely regarded as one of the most enchanting in the Adirondacks. I have paddled those confounding meanders many times, never tiring of each one's revelations.

The pleasures of this river are no secret to lovers of the out-of-doors. The wilderness stream has been popular for over a century. At one time, a hotel, the Inlet House, which belonged to George Sternberg, stood on the banks of the Oswegatchie, two miles above Wanakena. Herbert F. Keith writes about this area in his book, *Man of the Woods*. Keith describes visiting the Inlet House in 1907. The only way to get to the hotel was by an old wagon road from Star Lake or a trail along the river from Wanakena. At the time, Wanakena and the Rich Lumber Company lands were subject to the dry laws—but not Sternberg's, which boasted a fully licensed barroom.

The buildings along the Oswegatchie were removed following the purchase of the area for the state forest preserve. Keith offers the observation that although it was good for the river to be protected from logging, he still harbors fond memories of the days when one could travel the river stopping at the old guide camps and at the Inlet House for a hot meal at journey's end.

One of my favorite parts of Keith's book is his discussion of the old "Root Hole." There is no finer symbol, in my mind, of the timeless nature of the woods, of the slow way things change when man has little say in the matter. I can't improve on Keith's own description:

Magnificent white pines tower over the Oswegatchie River above High Falls. These trees were nearly all toppled by the fierce windstorm of 1995.

we arrived at a deep spot called the Root Hole, where an enormous pine root was embedded in sand. About 1911, this big stump with its octopus roots washed out of the bank in high water and trundled away. After hanging up on some alders and staying in place for about fifteen years, it resumed its slow journey downstream with each year's spring runoff. Finally, it reached the Inlet landing in the spring of 1967. At this writing [about 1971], it is still there, its roots providing many-leveled seats for picnickers about to launch their boats. Parts of it have been cut off for firewood. Someday it may float down through the rapids and reach Cranberry Lake.

Ever since reading this passage, I always muse about the progress of the various downed trees, old dock moorings, and so forth that I happen upon. Once attuned to looking for such things, return trips can become like visits to old friends not seen in a while. You recall that so-and-so had more hair the last time or that his waistline has gone a bit further south—or that the old Root Hole has moved another mile or two.

At this writing, following the furious windstorm of July 1995, the waters of the upper Oswegatchie are nearly impassable. The magnificent virgin pines that once marched along the banks above High Falls have toppled. Root holes like the one Keith described abound to confound the paddler. It is a sad time in the history of the river.

But one cannot think of a river as a static thing. As the seasons pass, it ages like a man, digging deeper into its banks, developing character even as its pace slows. Each individual trip upon a river is like a snapshot in time. But its true measure comes only when the still pictures are run together like the flip cards that show a racehorse running around a track. One day, the giant trees will again appear as the cards flip past.

A river, like a life, can never be fully measured until the course has been run to the end.

Monsters in the Woods

I am playing with my dolls—well, actually, my four-year-old daughter and I are playing with "her" dolls—when she comes up with a new game. She calls it, "Monsters in the Woods." She lines up all her favorite dolls on the floor and then picks out two of her more gruesome stuffed animals. These are the bad guys. My role is to "make the words" for the dolls who are supposed to scream and be terrified of the monsters.

This is great fun in the world of a four year old. But the whole exercise makes me think about a much more serious subject.

There have been a number of attacks on women in the area recently, some in wooded tracts and a few smack in the center of local campuses. Such attacks are hardly surprising anymore even in our relatively peaceful backwater. But having a daughter of one's own focuses the mind on the subject.

On a sunny, warm afternoon not long ago, and just a few days after the last rash of attacks made all the local papers, I went canoeing for a couple of hours on the Little River. To my considerable amazement, during this outing I saw no fewer than three coeds alone, deep in the woods, on a trail that is often used for jogging.

My first reaction was disbelief, followed by a sort of fatalistic "they must be nuts" feeling. But then I thought again.

What would it really be like to not be able to go out alone in the woods on a beautiful autumn day? As a man, I can hardly imagine the anger this exclusion from one of life's greatest joys must cause. I go into the woods or canoe up a stream alone almost daily. My life without this privilege would be nearly unthinkable.

And yet, it is a privilege that will likely be denied my daughter—if she is sensible. But if she is not, I must try to understand a little how she feels—try to understand the feelings that inspired the "take back the night" marches that have occurred all over the country. Maybe some of those women I saw out on that lonely trail were there because they simply refused to be intimidated.

I have tried to think of some situation where I have experienced the same kinds of feelings that women must experience all the time. And there is one. I am not a hunter, but I enjoy being in the woods most of all during hunting season. It is, after all, one of the most beautiful times to be there. But during hunting season, there is always in the back of my head a small fear. There is the knowledge that I am taking a risk, however slight. That knowledge makes me alter where I go, what I wear, how much noise I make, the time of day I go out, and so forth.

For two months every fall, I feel differently when I go into the woods or paddle up a stream. And I think for those two months I feel what women must feel all the time. It is not a pleasant feeling.

I don't have any answers. I don't know what can be done about it. It is one of life's many unfairnesses. But the problem makes me sad every time I look at my daughter and think about those many magic moments I have had alone in the woods. Moments she may never know.

There are no monsters in my woods.

And the Coyotes Shall Inherit the Earth

One of the funniest headlines I've seen in a long time went like this: "Coyotes Encroaching on Cities and Suburbs."

That caption no doubt belonged to some overworked editor who didn't even bother to read the story. For the writer in this case, Bill Marvel of the *Dallas Morning News*, also wrote: "As the suburbs spread out into coyote territory, the coyote, hard-pressed for food and living space, is increasingly moving into suburbia."

The writer understood what was going on and who was really doing the encroaching. But the way that headline read, one had to have visions of poor old suburbia being invaded by crazed coyotes. Can't you just see it? The packs moving into Westchester, crossing San Francisco's Golden Gate, or snuffling along cold and windy Lake Shore Drive in Chicago? Families running screaming through the streets like a scene out of *The Blob?* Coyotes swarming into Central Park, breakfasting at Tiffany's, or having a cold one at Tavern on the Green?

"Coyotes Encroaching on Cities and Suburbs." Enough to make your blood run cold.

More seriously, though, that newspaper banner signals a way of looking at the natural world that is both common and cockeyed. We are so cut off and so self-centered that we don't even question such a ridiculous headline.

What is natural here? Cities? Suburbs? These conglomerations of concrete, metal, glass, plastics, and toxic accretions of a thousand varieties are hardly natural. Only in one sense could they be so considered—as a result of their having been created by one of nature's own.

We are too far away from nature, living in our little boxes, packed in by the millions. It is time we recognized what we have done. Man is the one who has encroached on the rightful living space of all other living things. In the short run, those living things will suffer, but in the long run, man will also have to pay. We are enamored of our ability to adapt and to change our habitat, but the truth is, we are far less adaptable than many other creatures.

Those coyotes are doing what they have been programmed to do for millions of years—survive. And they are darn good at it. In his article, Bill Marvel quotes Richard Felosky, who has spent twenty-five years dealing with coyotes in Los Angeles, a city with thousands of the animals: "They're the smartest animal in the world. There's no way anybody in his right mind is thinking of eradicating this species or even controlling it very well."

Kind of puts things in perspective. Almighty man with his dart guns and computers and satellite tracking and high-tech traps and night-vision goggles can't even control Wile E. Coyote.

Maybe the coyote is trying to tell us something, something like "Stop encroaching on our lands, and we'll stop encroaching on yours." Just leave us a little space, that's all the creatures of this planet are saying.

I can tell you one thing for sure. Coyotes don't *want* to live in L.A. any more than the rest of us do.

Blue Horizons

I'm standing on top of a high ridge in New Hampshire. A ledge of
granite, wide and solid, stretches for almost a hundred feet clear of
trees. The view is staggering. Immediately before me lies the valley
of the Little Sugar River followed by ridge upon ridge of deep blue
mountains stretching to the horizon. The vista is dominated on one
side by the massive presence of Mount Ascutney, which is actually in
Vermont.

From this altitude, all is green. Or blue. It should be white of
course, this being New Year's Day, but we are already well into the
nineties, decade of global warming and ozone holes. Today, the view
is green. Or blue. No white in evidence.

If I lean just about as far out over the cliff as a normally acro-
phobic individual will hazard, I can see the house where I am staying.
Nestled in the green, it and a few others are the only ones visible in
all that majesty. That's an illusion, of course. There are plenty of other
homes and even villages down there, but altitude can hide a lot.

I've skied all through this particular forest. When my sister and
her boyfriend moved to this place on the edge of nothing ten years
ago, they were ecstatic at its isolation. Located at the top of an impos-
sibly steep dirt road, they and a handful of others share what is
known locally as "Straw Hill." How it got that name I have no idea,
but the name has certainly gained in accuracy since my sister arrived
to raise sheep and llamas.

Like most of New Hampshire, these woods tell a story of pioneer
settlement. Once, the hills were open and filled with roaming sheep
and cattle. I am still astonished when, after a full day of skiing higher

and deeper into these woods, I come upon a two-hundred-year-old foundation. Lines of stone fences that once marked fields, today wander off into the forest like lost and forgotten descendants of Hadrian's Wall.

But things have changed in the ten years since I first skied here.

Today, the path that once led steeply upward past the turn into my sister's yard has been scraped and graded. Its former surface of moss and lichens has been replaced by a muddy road that turns nearly impassable at the first rain. Beyond, the trail leading to the lookout has also been scarred. Bulldozer tracks carved into the ground half a dozen years ago remain clearly visible. Many magnificent trees—white pine, spruce, hemlock, and birch—have been cut. At first, these cuts created a parklike atmosphere, but the workers did not stay on to maintain the openness, and today the brush has returned with a vengeance. It has become an ugly landscape.

But the real tragedy is that all of this destruction was performed on speculation. Here was a beautiful spot, all were agreed, and the developers roared in with visions of greenbacks dancing before their eyes. No sooner were the roads built and the trees cut, however, than the real estate boom of the eighties ground to an abrupt halt. What has been left behind is nothing less than a raped landscape. The owners even abandoned derelict automobiles and mobile homes high up on the sides of formerly wild mountains. It is enough to make you cry.

It is enough to make you wonder how anyone could ever choose to leave our dwindling wild lands to the mercy of the uncontrolled developer.

I Have an Old Pickup Truck

I have an old pickup truck. It is in its eleventh year, has one entire side bashed in where someone ran a stop sign and struck me several years ago, and has an odometer that will never see the south side of 150,000 miles again. I use the aging beast only occasionally during the winter. I am trying to stretch out its golden years because I can't afford a replacement.

When I went out and fired it up last week after nearly two winter months without moving, it responded immediately and roared to life. But as I watched the billowing clouds of oil smoke and steam, I felt a distinct twinge of guilt. This vehicle is clearly one of the ones legislators had in mind when they began to call for new regulations to inspect and remove from the road old cars and trucks that are polluting far in excess of what they should.

As I watched the carbons drift upward to contribute their share to greenhouse warming and ozone holes and even to deforestation and species depletion, I felt with utter clarity the tugging conflicts of our age.

I need that truck for a hundred chores in any given year. It is freely lent to friends who are moving or who have purchased a new piano or who need help in their woodlot. If I did not have it handy whenever I needed it, I would be forever on the phone trying to borrow or rent or hire its replacement.

My need for that truck has compromised my environmental principles. And the truth is, we all do this on a depressingly regular basis. I write frequently about how we are not doing enough to protect our planet, and I believe in the importance of that message. But I am as guilty as any, simply by participating in modern society.

I am usually the last one to go to bed in my family at night. Just walking about the house turning out the lights and appliances sometimes takes several minutes. Electric lights, VCR, television, outdoor halogen light, power switch to gas heater, computer, overhead living room fan. Then I turn on a few night lights and go to bed. I am actually quite aware of excessive electric use and when I am home alone rarely have anything on that I don't need. But my wife has a different priority—she likes a home that looks lived in, with lots of lights inviting friends to stop by and dissuading burglars from doing the same. I cannot blame her for having her own priorities—after all, I have that truck.

People are much more conscious of these things than they used to be. Our environmental awareness has been raised significantly over the last twenty years. We can see the evidence everywhere, from recycling programs to greater use of solar and wind power to increased insulation and lead-free gasoline. New regulations, like the ones to control my truck, appear every year forcing ever greater conservation efforts.

We would seem to be making progress. But it is a daunting, grudging, glacial sort of progress. We are engaged in endless compromise in order to maintain our lifestyles. And as we add one billion people to this earth every ten years, it grows increasingly difficult to see how we can keep up, let alone get ahead of the curve.

Population growth is our nemesis. Every day we add the population equivalent of Rochester, New York, to the planet. I used to live in Rochester. It's a nice city. But no way do we need 365 more Rochesters every year. Since most of the increase is in the third world, a better example would be that we are adding an entire Mexico every year. Another India every decade.

Only the blindest observers could believe that our puny conservation efforts will be enough to meet this challenge. And as I head outside to fire up my truck once more, the enormity of the beast we have created weighs heavily on my mind.

Losing Touch

Earlier, I wrote about the differing perceptions of a racing cross-country skier and a couple of bird watchers. Although they were both clearly enjoying themselves, there was still a distinct contrast between their experiences. Without a doubt, the bird watchers were interacting with their surroundings in a more intimate manner.

Increasingly, humans appear to be altering their psychic relationship with the out-of-doors. It is rare to see someone out in the natural world simply for the sake of being there, for the pure enjoyment of feeling one is a part of the forest or lake or mountain. Today, we have to be there for a reason—to improve our "time" as we race through the landscape on foot or by ski or to get a thrill by riding a machine, be it snowmobile, dirt bike, speedboat or hang glider.

When was the last time you actually saw a poet or musician or artist out practicing his or her craft alone in the woods? When was the last time you saw anyone simply walking? Walking has become the health craze of the nineties. The highways are filled with "serious" walkers, many of them wired for sound, working hard at the business of extending their life spans (yet another *reason* to justify being in the outdoors). Most can be seen along busy highways where the rumble of trucks and the stench of diesel fuel must surely detract from the experience and probably from the health benefits as well. No doubt many are forced to this by constraints of time and work, but it is a sad spectacle nonetheless.

Most of us seem not to have a clue why we should be in the out-of-doors. We need an excuse, as though there could be no conceivable benefit to simply being there. How far away we have traveled from the place that produced us!

And yet, is it really all that surprising? One recent government study found that Americans on average spend 93 percent of their time indoors, only 2 percent outdoors and 5 percent in transit between the two. And how much of that paltry 2 percent is actually quality outdoor time spent communing with nature? I suspect most of it is filled with things like mowing the lawn or playing in the company softball game.

And what of our kids? Philosophers love to speculate that children are much closer to the spirit of natural man, unspoiled at three and five and nine years of age. What could be more beautiful, what could fill our hearts more than the sight of a child running in the woods or staring in wonder at a deer or a waterfall?

But today's child may well be outdoors even less than his stressed-out parent. Children spend an average of two hours a day playing video games and perhaps another four or more watching TV. By the time they are five or six, they have seen thousands of commercials and have participated in the video deaths of an equal number of aliens, Indians, robots, and turtles.

Small wonder that the natural world is disappearing so rapidly when most of us seem to have so little interest in it. Small wonder that we refuse to adequately provide for the upkeep of our national parks. Small wonder that for three years running New York State was unable to find a tiny amount of money to protect its most beautiful pieces of landscape.

Very small wonder indeed.

Eating the Earth

This is the Age of Information, which may be my problem. There's an awful lot to worry about these days. Most people don't take their worrying seriously. For example, have you ever noticed how people are always claiming to be optimists? When was the last time you heard someone brag that he was a pessimist at heart? No one wants to admit it. But a poet once said, "Pessimism, when you get used to it, is just as agreeable as optimism." So I've decided to come out of the closet.

I worry. A lot.

To give you an idea, here's a typical conversation between my wife and me. Setting the scene: my wife is sitting on the couch reading Charlotte Brontë's latest potboiler. I rush into the room, turn on the TV, and perch on the edge of my chair.

Warily, she says, "What is it now?"

"Carl Sagan," I whisper breathlessly. "He's discussing the likelihood of a certain comet striking the planet."

"Mmm." Her eyes droop.

"This could be it," I say. "I think we should do something."

"What?"

"I don't know—cancel our cable service, close out the IRA, pack a suitcase."

"Sorry. My end-of-the-world outfit is at the cleaners till Tuesday. Do you think you could call Carl and ask him to postpone?"

Cynicism is the first defense of all unimaginative people.

I honestly don't know why I am so interested in disaster. Granted, the news is full of impending doom from the creeping deserts of Africa to the decimation of the rhino for the cure of impotence in Asia (hard to believe they could possibly have any). Yet my friends don't seem to be similarly focused, and my wife considers me positively macabre at this point, almost afraid to bring me out when the guests arrive—"He's in the den, charting the progress of the fire-ant invasion."

I am riveted by the latest reports of skin cancer among the shepherds of Tierra del Fuego from the growing ozone hole. Leaking gas storage tanks in the ground in the Midwest make me want to distill every drop of water that passes my lips. A brother-in-law who calls to brag about new ocean-front property he has just purchased is quickly put in his place by my declaration that melting polar ice caps will soon render his investment into ocean-bottom property.

At parties, I decry the deforestation of Brazil to provide these trendy chopsticks. The depletion of species, I pontificate, will certainly doom us to some as yet unknown and horrible disease whose only cure would have been the crushed tongues of extinct Amazonian treetoads.

Why do I devour this stuff? Why do any of us? I know I'm not alone. Despite the chuckles from guests as my wife informs them that I've just installed a hot line to Ralph Nader, I know I'm not the only one who buys those hundreds of environmental newsmagazines or who watches the endless stream of television specials about denuded forests in Haiti.

The simple truth is, it's interesting—kind of like that story about the starving man who begins to eat his own body in order to survive. It's horrible, but so fascinating you can't wait to find out the ending. Does he eat himself all up before he's rescued or not? Will we humans eat up our planet before we are rescued?

The difference, of course, is that we've got to rescue ourselves.

California Gold

Not far from my home, there is a stand of gray birch that guards the edge of a meadow. At a certain moment every evening, the pale bark catches the glow of the sun. It is most stirring after a heavy thunderstorm when the black clouds part, sending rays of gold marching into the trees. These particular birches are not imposing. They do not tower against the sky or sway gracefully like the tall, neighboring tamarack. They are a small cluster, no more than twenty-five feet in height, but what they lack in size, they more than make up for in spirit.

The gray birch is a spirited tree in many regards. My nearby stand is frequently assaulted by high winds. After a storm, the dead branches and limbs and entire trees lean against each other or on the ground in all manner of disarray. It is as though some all-powerful being had been playing pickup sticks with them. Yet, before long, most of the leaning limbs have made their way to the forest floor and the rest of the stand seems to renew itself.

In its ability to play with light, the birch has no equal. The silver bark, delicate limbs, and feathery leaves make much of the sunlight that reaches them. Their beauty against a background of black storm clouds is otherworldly, and the wind-rattled leaves remind one of the twinkling lights of some distant port city as seen from shipboard. "The light of these trees," Thoreau wrote, "affects me more than California gold."

I have been equally impressed, while skiing the high country of our eastern mountains, by the paper birch. As I work my way up through forests of pine or spruce or maple, the trees suddenly appear coinciding with an increased openness of landscape. Perhaps only a small stand at first, but growing in number as I ski onward, they soon fill a bowl of low hills or march glowingly across a hillside. These fine specimens, possibly the result of wildfire that burned all in its path down to the bare mineral soil, may be eighteen inches in diameter with three or four boles sprouting at once from a single spot on the forest floor. In a day's outing of many miles, I pass through dozens of such birch woods, each with its own character and each clearly remembered on the return journey.

It seems a travesty that such a tree should have so many human uses. Humans, after all, rarely need any excuse at all to cut down a tree. The paper birch has been used for roofing improvised shelters, building canoes, snowshoes, paddles, and toboggans, brewing tea, making syrup and sugar, and for treating chapped lips and gonorrhea. The rolled bark can even serve as a candle or as a vessel to boil water. The inner bark was ground and used as an emergency flour during hard winters. Birchbark shoes, hats, rope, and clothing were commonly used in Scandinavia at the turn of the century.

William O. Douglas, in his book, *My Wilderness: East to Katahdin*, describes an unusual use for the bark of the birch: "This bark also makes excellent horns for the calling of moose. An old Indian guide I knew would, after making his calls on the birchbark horn, dip it in the lake, fill it with water, and then pour the water back in the lake to simulate the urination of a cow. 'Thees make old moose come fast,' he would say."

Yet for all of this practicality, James Russell Lowell labeled the birch, "most shy and ladylike of trees."

The gentle birch remains one of our most lovely forest specimens. In its movement, we can witness a perfectly balanced part of nature. For the birch is the very essence of a windy day.

Heaven's Lace

I stare in amazement as perhaps the twentieth flock of Canada geese soars over my head. For whatever reason, the place where I am hiking, along a riverbank outside of the tiny North Country village of Madrid, is alive with the sights and sounds of these birds. Only once before have I witnessed so many geese, while on a canoe trip in northern Quebec. On that occasion, the entire sky was filled with birds making haste in their fluidly changing Vs.

Today, the first flock to attract my attention with its raucous cries turns out to also be the most beautiful. It is actually a double V—two huge open-ended triangles of birds, one inside the other. As I stare at them, they pass high overhead and into a position that allows their bodies to reflect the sun. Suddenly they begin to shimmer, almost like the rippling surface of a lake reflecting the sunlight. It is incredibly beautiful, a shimmering series of golden ribbons floating across the sky. The ribbons open and close, form loops, the two open triangles combine into one, then separate again.

I am witnessing one of nature's marvelous random patterns. The Vs change constantly, subject to the whims of air currents, individual birds' waning or waxing strengths, and perhaps a host of other factors unknown to me. The central truth of their movement is the peek-aboo, now you see it, now you don't, V-shape. The arrowhead form is obviously the best for parting the waves of the airstream. I note how hard the leaders work in comparison to those birds farther back. The laggards seem to float effortlessly with only occasional wing action. Soon, the leader tires and is replaced. This constant replacement of the commander in chief is yet another factor in the continuous alteration of the pattern.

The magnificent double triangle lasts but a few moments, replaced first by one huge V, then by a sort of inverted C, then back to a V that slowly closes across the back side until there is a nearly perfect, closed triangle floating across the sky. Almost as soon as I realize that I am witnessing a bit of tenth-grade geometry in the heavens, the triangle dissipates and the entire flock seems to suddenly lose its co-ordinating grace. For a few moments there is no discernable pattern at all. The birds struggle to regain their natural rhythm. "Who's in charge here?" I can almost hear one of them crying. Their honking grows even more contentious, as though they had suddenly deterio-rated into a squabbling meeting of the local school board.

Finally, at the edge of my ability to see them, they appear to at last get it all right again, and I see a distant, shimmering V disappear into the clouds. The moment they are gone, another flock calls behind me, and then another, and another. I try to estimate their numbers. In little more than ten minutes, at least a thousand have passed overhead.

But it is that first image of a shimmering, golden, and, yes, squab-bling V, evaporating into the stratosphere that I will never forget. What, I wonder, do such creatures discuss in such strident terms as they float across the heavens? Is it conceivable that they are unable to divine their own beauty?

No doubt, for as Emerson has observed: "All the thoughts of a turtle are turtle."

Canada

That untrav'lled world whose margins fade forever and forever
—FROM THE JOURNAL OF PETER POND

The Maritimes

I once read about a sea kayaking adventure in the icy straits of Chichago Island near Glacier Bay in southeast Alaska. The writer related a fascinating wilderness trip marked by encounters with enormous brown bears and campsites bordered by climax forests of 350-year-old Sitka spruce and Western hemlock. The adventure was made all the more memorable for its participants by some eight inches of rainfall in five days (not all that unusual for the area).

More outdoor writing has been done about Alaska than perhaps any other place in the world. For a time, it seemed as though any writer worth his salt had to have a book out on the wonders of our largest state. There was John McPhee and Joe McGinnis and, of course, James Michener, to name but a handful.

Never having been to Alaska, I must admit I would not turn down the opportunity. I have no doubts as to its incredible beauties. But it is, after all, four to five thousand miles away. We have some equally beautiful country on this side of the continent. The place I have in mind may not be terra firma U.S. soil and it may not have the equal of Alaska's mountains nor her brown bears and grizzlies. But it is nonetheless magnificent, and it certainly boasts a richer history.

I have pondered for years why more attention is not paid to northeastern Canada. Perhaps it is too close for us to feel we have truly got out into the bush. After all, much of this wilderness is little more than a three-hour flight from at least a hundred million people. Northern Quebec, Labrador, and Newfoundland offer a wide variety of wilderness experience, not to mention a fascinating history extending back nearly one thousand years to the first Vikings who landed at L'Anse aux Meadows on the northern tip of the island of Newfoundland.

It is also a place that has not been done to death by writers. Although there is an extensive literature of exploration, in recent times only Farley Mowat leaps to mind as a writer whose work truly encompasses the region. Mowat's books range north to the Arctic, but he has clearly chosen the Gulf of St. Lawrence and the surrounding maritime provinces and islands as one part of the world he values highly. In *Sea of Slaughter,* he encyclopedically documents how man has been systematically destroying the wildlife of the region ever since the first whalers made landfall off the coasts of Greenland and Labrador around the year 1500.

If ever there was a case history that should be studied by environmentalists as they battle to save Alaska's wild places, it is Mowat's book. Alaska has been saved thus far (with the notable exceptions of Prince William Sound and the pipeline areas of the tundra) primarily because of its remoteness. But that remoteness has been receding rapidly. Despite the large areas supposedly set aside for parks, wetlands, and wilderness, it sometimes seems as though politicians from the governor's mansion to the White House are eyeing Alaska's mineral wealth. They do so with a greedy disregard to the damage already being done to this final true wilderness left in the United States.

When I was growing up in the fifties and sixties, Alaska was the place to go. I remember high school friends whose parents packed them up and moved to the remotest parts of the big state never to be heard from again—at least by me. It sometimes seemed everyone I knew, at one time or another, made a hegira to Alaska. I cannot tell you how many slide shows I sat through of old 1950s Buicks and Oldsmobiles, roofs disappearing under loads of army surplus tenting, as they huffed their way up the Alaska highway.

But reading that story on sea kayaking made me realize what a paradise we have right under our own noses. The rocky coastlines of Nova Scotia, Newfoundland, and Labrador offer thousands of miles (over four thousand miles in Nova Scotia alone) of fascinating and historically vital shores, of countless offshore islands, of fiords with thousand-foot cliffs, of seals, seabirds, moose, caribou, and whales.

It's all there for the taking or—more aptly—for the experiencing. And I guarantee you that for every individual you come across who will be able to say to your tales, "Oh, I've been there," there will be ten such if you go to Alaska.

Fire and Brimstone

We are out on Quoddy Bay, a mile offshore on the eastern coast of Nova Scotia. The night is very clear and the ocean dead calm. Loons are calling all around us, their warbling echoing across the water from island to island. In our first half-hour on this primordial evening, we have seen terns, osprey, eider ducks, cormorants, herons, herring gulls, great black-backed gulls, Canada geese, and a bald eagle. As well as the loons.

It is a feast of bird life. They seem to have figured out that this place is teeming with the things they like: clams, mussels, scallops, and sea cucumbers in the shallows; mackerel, eel, and bait fish farther out. A local fisherman gives us a bucket full of large mussels. He stares out at a clutch of black cormorants on a rock, their scrawny necks sticking up like so many headless toadstools. "Shags," he says, spitting the word out in distaste. "Junk birds." He dislikes them because they represent competition for the shellfish.

The setting sun is bright behind us. We don't want to paddle into it and so are drawn farther out to sea as we await its fall behind the towering headland of Brimstone. All around are islands, low pebbled ones that all but disappear at high tide, steeply cliffed ones topped with ragged spruce, twisted corkscrew ones with banks of bone-white driftwood, and massive balancing rocks perched on smooth, Precambrian granite. The light strikes them all with an ethereal, golden glow.

It is easy to get disoriented and lost out here. Hundreds of islands stretch along this section of eastern shore. The coastline itself is tortured, glacially torn with deep, fiordlike bays and long, spitted points reaching far out to sea.

We have the latest government map for this section of coast.

There is a new designation offshore that was not on our old maps: The Eastern Shore Islands Wildlife Management Area. Stretching along some forty miles of coast reaching out a dozen miles from the mainland, its boundaries appear to have been drawn by some graph-happy physicist—right angles jutting out in all directions, attempting to include a wide variety of islands. From tiny Black Peg and Pumpkin on the west to Little Goose and Tuffin to the east, it is one varied and beautiful place for sea kayaking.

At last the sun settles behind Brimstone. We have passed beyond the farthest island in our straight-line passage away from Sol's bright light. Now we rest facing the open ocean and feel the large swells that have made their way some thousands of miles across the North Atlantic in order to make our tiny craft rise and fall here in this spot.

As soon as the sun sets, the light begins to disappear rapidly. We have a long way to go back to Quoddy wharf. Turning our boats toward the mainland, everything now looks unfamiliar—the islands are dark and indistinguishable from each other, the passages between them no longer discernible against the night. For a moment, I feel rising trepidation and wonder if we may have to spend the night bobbing out here on the North Atlantic. But instead, we strike a new course for Quoddy Head, an elongated cape that sticks far out into the ocean. Once sighted, it becomes a simple matter to follow the shoreline even in the dark.

A sliver of moon emerges. The sky is still remarkably blue, making the blackness of the ocean surface and islands seem only more intense. The light does strange things here at dusk. Above, a jet spreads its contrail as it seems to climb straight up to the moon: image of a hammer and sickle in the sky.

Nearing the wharf where we began, we stop paddling and float. There is a sense of suspension between inky black sea and the vast, darkening sky. It is very still and quiet. Even the loons have stopped calling. The last light before nightfall bathes the surroundings a deep crimson.

For only the thousandth time in my life, I wish I were an artist. This place cries out for a paintbrush. And I can only write about it—in black and white.

Moratorium

On July 2, 1992, the Canadian government announced a two-year moratorium on the northern cod fishery in Newfoundland. A total of nineteen thousand fishermen suddenly found themselves out of work. Because of the timing of the announcement from Ottawa, most of the fishing boats had just been completely fitted out for the coming season, making an additional financial burden.

Trouble in the cod fishery has been around for a long time, and it was clear by 1992 that the government had waited too long to address the problem. Years ago, I wrote about the decline I had witnessed in the number of cod fishermen in Nova Scotia where I have vacationed for forty years. But the summer of 1991 produced a disastrous fishery following colder-than-normal ocean temperatures and the worst ice conditions in living memory. Scientists say, however, that any link between the weather conditions and the ocean harvest can only be speculation, as no one has seen any dead fish. The cod simply disappeared. In fact, there is now little doubt that the main causes are overfishing and high-tech vessels rather than ecological factors. Many are in denial of this truth. It is, perhaps, human nature to look for scapegoats. One such has been the harbor seal, which is often blamed for taking too many fish and which has actually been shot in growing numbers by angry citizens.

Scientists assessing the northern cod stocks in June 1992 reported a sharp decline since 1990 to record low levels. Inshore catches had fallen from fourteen thousand tons in the early 1980s to just five hundred tons. Fishermen in Cape Breton and on the southwest coast of Newfoundland say that the desperate state of their cod stocks warrants an expansion of the moratorium both in duration (to three years) and extent (to include Nova Scotia waters). (Since this was written, the moratorium has been extended indefinitely throughout the Maritimes).

Meanwhile, government support payments to out-of-work fishermen will amount to more than $500 million through 1995. That is not good news for the rocky Canadian economy. Other fish stocks also need a "rest" from heavy fishing pressures. Federal scientists report that haddock and pollock stocks off Nova Scotia are being fished at more than twice the level they should be.

But it is also true that ecological factors are at least contributing to the demise of Canada's fisheries. For generations, we have been using the oceans of the world as a vast repository for the wastes and toxics of industrial society. Most fish live in the rich waters near the continents, generally within two hundred miles of shore. They are subject to all manner of pollutants from sewage runoff to nuclear waste junkyards under the sea. PCB's and dioxins, two of the most toxic substances known to man, are so pervasive in the environment that minute quantities can be found in any fish in the world. As many as eighteen toxic chemicals have been found in tuna samples that were inspected and "passed" by the United States Food and Drug Administration. The overwhelmed FDA only tests fish for fourteen of the thousands of chemicals in the environment.

Meanwhile, bad news continues to show up where it is least expected. It has been revealed that the Baltic Sea is a repository of Nazi World War II chemical weapons, and the former Soviet Union disclosed a vast nuclear dumping ground in the Arctic of radioactive materials, including several reactors from scuttled submarines. Already, say Russian and Swedish environmentalists, these dumping grounds have caused many deaths and injuries to fishermen.

So a moratorium on the cod fishery of Newfoundland should not come as a surprise to anyone. It may even be more of a surprise that something—however belatedly—is finally being done about it.

Back in the 1860s, when moose were disappearing from the Adirondacks, far from trying to address the problem, our ancestors took part in a madcap contest to see who could shoot the "last" moose. Controversy over who might actually claim "credit" for that final kill went on for decades.

We seem to have come a small step forward from that pre-ecological age. No one today is trying to claim credit for the last cod. In that tiny triumph may well lie the future of mankind.

Voyageur

The story of the voyageurs has been told and retold until it has taken on heroic dimensions. Yet superlatives are often necessary in any attempt to describe the incredible hardships that these men endured— and endured not just with good humor but often with a song on their lips.

They used canoes that could carry three or four tons of cargo and were powered by eight to ten men. The Montreal canoe was thirty-five to forty feet in length. It was made from the bark of the yellow birch, which was placed over ribs of white cedar. The bark was then secured by melted pine gum. This gum was easily attainable and thus repairs could be quickly made almost anywhere—a good thing because the boats leaked constantly.

The engagés, the paid voyageurs of the fur-trading companies, often traveled eighteen hours a day and could maintain a stroke rate during that time of one per second with only a few stops. Such rest breaks were called "pipes," for obvious reasons.

During portages, each man carried a minimum of 180 pounds across his back supported by a tumpline, a leather strap that bound the pack and rested on the carrier's forehead. It was not unheard of for a man to carry two or even three hundred pounds at a time. With this weight, they *jogged* across the portage routes, which were usually little more than breaks in the underbrush. All of this was carried out, of course, at the height of the blackfly and mosquito seasons.

There are many descriptions of the voyageurs going about their incredible labors by travelers who were conveyed by the boatmen. It was often said that these unencumbered "guests" could not keep up with the pace the voyageurs maintained as they ran through the woods weighted down by their enormous packs.

The voyageurs were extremely competitive—a natural enough phenomenon given the fact that time was money for them in much the same way that it is for today's truckers. In one documented race that took place on Lake Winnipeg, the men paddled all out for forty-eight consecutive hours without a halt.

Yet these were not supermen. In fact, they were a very small breed of man, thick set, active, and usually no more than 5'5" in height. If they grew much taller than this, they found it impossible to fit their legs into the canoes. As a general rule, they died young, after suffering many agonizing injuries, from herniated disks to weakened and torn knees and backs.

The diet upon which the voyageurs performed their miracles of stamina was a sickening mix of often rotted salt pork and pemmican. They were called *mangers de lard* by those who witnessed their fetid feasts. Occasionally, if they had time, they would supplement their diet with fish or hunted game, but time was scarce in the lives of the voyageurs.

These were largely uneducated men. Young Canadians expected to earn their living on the rivers, and there was no time for school. In 1800, it was estimated that not one boy in five could write his own name. Nearly all the voyageurs signed their contracts with an X.

It was a brutal life. The winters were the worst time of all. Perhaps two thousand miles from his home base, a trapper might spend the long winter alone, though many took Indian wives. If game was scarce, starvation and dysentery was his likely fate.

Yet despite the hardships, the voyageurs were men of fierce pride who sang hearty songs about their lives as they paddled their bateaux. For they were at least free men in a wild land, and, for the short span of their lives, many felt themselves luckier than their fellows.

Bogs

Behind the small cottage my family has in Nova Scotia is a series of large bogs. They cover many acres, interrupted occasionally by patches of spruce or small pools of water called tarns. Growing up with these mystical places out my back door was like having my own never-neverland. It was a magic kingdom bound only by spruce dangling gray gossamers of moss flown in on the capricious winds of the North Atlantic.

The surface of a bog is soft and squishy, covered with a cornucopia of plants—orchids, ferns, leatherleaf, pitcher plants, Labrador tea, and bakeapples, also known as cloudberries. My sister and I would spend hours tramping about, our bare feet sinking as much as two feet into the muck. We picked berries by the gallon, went swimming in the "bottomless" tarns, and sneaked up on deer feeding on the berries. Sometimes the fog from the ocean rolled in across the bays and headlands, creating an eerie landscape, and we were warned often against getting too far out on the bogs where it was easy to get disoriented.

I have a great affection for these places and was glad to learn recently that there are more than a billion acres of bogs on the planet. More than 4 percent of the earth's landmass is covered in peat, and because bogs hold vast amounts of carbon, they are being closely studied to determine their effects on global warming.

The United States and Canada have huge peat deposits, in contrast to much of Europe, where peat has been mined for centuries for fuel. The Netherlands, Germany, and Denmark have virtually no virgin bogs left. Finland has drained 45 percent of its bogs and Ireland more than 75 percent.

Controversy rages over the draining of bogs. Ecologists consider them rich repositories of plant life in delicate balance with their environment. And although peat is accumulating much faster than it is being used up in North America, many fragile boglands have been seriously hurt by development and harvesting.

Given my own long-term intimacy with bogs, I am always surprised when someone declares that they are nothing more than undesirable, wet, treeless "swamps." Some people can see no use in anything that can not be successfully turned into a dollar. Bogs have often been dismissed as a form of leprosy infecting the Canadian hinterland, a decaying muckland tormented by black flies and mosquitos.

I used to go out across the bogs picking bakeapples with my grandfather when he was ninety. Still vigorous, he tramped across acres of terrain carrying a huge bucket. Invariably, he picked more berries than I. He seemed to have a knack for knowing the best spots, no doubt the result of having picked these same bogs for nearly ninety years.

The tarns where my sister and I went swimming were generally avoided by the local population more or less out of superstition and the belief that they were bottomless, dangerous, and perhaps even alive with strange creatures. I still clearly recall the first time I ventured into one of them as a boy. I felt I was breaking all sorts of taboos and was deliciously scared. But in we dove anyway and, wonder of wonders, the water was warm. Here, by the frigid North Atlantic in which no one swam, was a perfect swimming hole, and none of the local residents made use of it. We would dive down and swim underneath the bog mat into a surreal world of floating debris and dangling roots.

Scrambling in and out of the tarns was a difficult and scratchy affair because of the loose, mushy sides. On more than one occasion, I thought I might not get out without the help of my companion. Small wonder mothers scared their children away. Once, we tried to plumb the largest tarn in our area and never could find the bottom. There is usually some basis in fact, apparently, for most superstitions.

Mackenzie's Trek

When I am carrying a canoe over a difficult spot or when I am loading my craft for a lengthy trip, I sometimes think of one Alexander Mackenzie, the wilderness explorer and miracle worker of the 1700s. Whatever hardships I imagine I am experiencing at the moment become little short of an embarrassment in comparison with Mackenzie's exploits.

Mackenzie's first trip in the effort to find a passage to the Pacific Ocean was, in his own mind, a miserable failure. In 1789, he and his men followed the river that today bears his name all the way to the Arctic Ocean. That incredible three-thousand-mile round-trip journey followed the course of a river whose main stream is longer than that of the Mississippi. Its vast and beautiful watershed links three great lakes and over thirty thousand square miles of blue water. But in Mackenzie's mind it was all nothing but a mistake. He even labeled the mighty concourse the "River of Disappointment."

In 1793, following two years in London learning astronomy and the art of taking bearings with a sea captain's instruments, Mackenzie was ready to try again to find a way to the Pacific. This time his crew consisted of six French-Canadian paddlers called *les voyageurs des bois*, two Indians, and one other white man.

The group constructed a magnificent birchbark canoe that was twenty-five feet long, had a four foot nine inch beam, and was twenty-six inches deep. Birchbark is a very tough material and one that is relatively easy to repair in the wild. It is also remarkably lightweight. This last quality was of no small concern given that the route the men would follow had one rather significant carry—the Rocky Mountains.

According to a description by Rutherford Platt in *The Great American Forest*, this boat carried a cargo of three thousand pounds, including a ton of food. Among the items loaded were sixteen ninety-pound bags of pemmican (dried cakes of chopped moosemeat mixed with fat, crushed berries, and fruits), six hundred pounds of corn, flour, rice, and sugar, one-fifth of a pint of rum per man per day, arms, ammunition, presents for the Indians, axes, canoe-building tools, moose hides for making moccasins, and Mackenzie's astronomical instruments.

The trip would turn into one more arduous than any in the group could have imagined. Setting off from Fort Chipewyan on Lake Athabasca, the voyageurs traveled up the Peace River. What began as an easy paddle turned into a nightmare as the Peace headed straight into the Rockies, eventually petering out in a gorge with massive walls and tumultuous glacial runoff. The men were forced to portage their gear and craft over the mountains, eventually crossing the Continental Divide. They relaunched on a steep mountain stream that hurled them down against boulders and fallen trees. Their strong birchbark canoe was wrecked before they reached the valley floor.

Building another canoe in just four days, the men continued on the Fraser River, where they came across Indians who lived in elaborate log lodges some thirty by forty feet in size. These Indians had never seen a white man. It was the first known encounter between white men and a Rocky Mountain Indian tribe.

Had Mackenzie continued down the Fraser, it would have taken him easily to the ocean at the site of present-day Vancouver. But he had no way of knowing this. Instead, on the advice of the Indians, he and his men retraced their steps back up the Fraser some sixty miles and proceeded to follow a tortuous, boulder-strewn stream that led them to further exhausting overland ordeals. In the end, they finally made it to the Pacific only to face a run-in with local Indians that very nearly cost Mackenzie his life.

After a total of just seventy-four days, Mackenzie's band of ten men completed their incredible round trip from Fort Chipewyan to the Pacific and back again. They had covered 1,200 miles, 940 miles by canoe, 260 miles backpacking overland.

As one might expect, it never became a popular route. To this day, no one has ever repeated the precise journey, and Mackenzie's fame has faded as a result of his failure to find—even for a canoe—the fabled northwest passage.

Hubbard

There are many sad stories of exploration in the Canadian North—stories of excruciating hardship, starvation, and misery. It is hard for us to imagine setting forth into such vast emptiness where no help of any kind can be expected. Even to do so today can be a daunting experience, although our modern age of seaplanes and radios and even satellites that can pinpoint a lost man's position within feet has taken much of the risk out of such an adventure.

But at the turn of the century, it took hardy souls indeed. Two such who shared a journey of starvation and mishap were Dillon Wallace and Leonidas Hubbard. Along with their Cree Indian guide, George Elson, they journeyed by canoe into the little-known region of Labrador from Hamilton Inlet to Lake Michikamau.

The expedition was the brainchild of Hubbard, who longed to see these lands only rarely visited by white men. They would traverse an uncharted wilderness in 1903 that was eventually destined to become the source of enormous amounts of late twentieth-century hydro-electric power. But adventure was their primary objective.

In the end, Hubbard gave his life for his adventure. A stirring account of their journey, *The Lure of the Labrador Wild,* was later written by Dillon Wallace as a memorial to his friend's indefatigable spirit. It was an account of a tragedy that might have been avoided but for an incredible bit of bad luck.

Their scheduled route to Michikamau lay along the Naskaupi River, which empties into Grand Lake. They had been told that the Naskaupi River entered a bay at the end of Grand Lake. But when they approached the bay into which the Naskaupi flowed, they were struck with indecision. Grand Lake itself continued on ahead of them, enticing them away from their correct route. It seemed unlikely that this bay they should have entered could be the correct one, for it was clearly not at the end of the lake as they had been repeatedly told.

According to Wallace's later description, Hubbard stood up in the canoe at this point for a better view of the bay and said, "Oh, that's just a bay and it isn't worth while to take time to explore it. The river comes in here at the end of the lake. They all said it was at the end of the lake." In fact, the mouth of the Naskaupi is divided by an island into two small streams. The island is heavily wooded and from the bay entrance no sign of the river can be seen.

And so, they entered another wide-mouthed river known as the Susan, which was to eventually lead them far off course. Their mistake was understandable. Grand Lake actually receives four rivers at its west end in bays of almost equal size. In most cases, a single large river leaving the end of a bay will alone drain the region. But here was an exception to the rule.

Although the men had a sextant, it was apparently not used at this point. The reason? They had no inkling of their mistake. The Susan was roughly the same size and bore the same sort of rapids that they had been told to expect on the Naskaupi.

By the time they realized their blunder, Dillon and Hubbard were far off-course in a land that did not suffer mistakes easily. The Labrador summer at these high latitudes is very short, and winter caught them unprepared. They never reached Lake Michikamau, although they were able to see it briefly, far in the distance, after climbing a high promontory.

The return journey brought hunger and incredible hardship. Hubbard, suffering from dysentery, grew progressively weaker until he was unable to continue. Wallace and Elson left him with their tent, firewood, and their remaining pitiful bits of food while they made a dash for help. But Hubbard died of exposure and starvation before they returned.

In his final diary entry, Hubbard wrote, "I am not suffering. The acute pangs of hunger have given way to indifference. I'm sleepy. I think death from starvation is not so bad. But let no one suppose I expect it. I am prepared—that is all."

Dry Newfoundland

My canoeing cohort of long standing called up the other day to give me my annual "We ought to go back to Newfoundland" pep talk. This has been something of a ritual ever since our trip several years ago to what was formerly Britain's oldest colony. On that occasion, we made one of the biggest mistakes of our paddling careers—we took along our canoes.

The trouble was that we had chosen one of the worst drought years in recent memory. Virtually all of the rivers we passed along the western shore of the island were bone dry. The only exception was the wide Humber River, a world-famous Mecca for salmon fishermen. And—you guessed it—we let the Humber pass in our haste to get to the really good stuff farther on. Although we continued our trip all the way up the western coast and beyond to L'Anse-Aux-Meadows, we were never able to float our canoes.

What we did discover, however, was some of the most spectacular and enticing coastline for kayaking that we had ever seen. Thus our despair at having brought canoes instead of our sea kayaks, which we had left behind in Nova Scotia. We felt like true rocket scientists as we drove past spectacular fiords with sheer rock cliffs rising hundreds of feet from the ocean. The intricate coastline boasted beautiful coves, small fishing villages, and remote points thrusting into the Gulf of St. Lawrence in an area known for its whales. Through it all, our Mad River canoe sat high and dry on our rooftop, mocking us.

Still, it was hard not to fall in love with the province despite our disappointment. We spent two days at Gros Morne National Park,

An unusually placid scene on the stormy North Atlantic.

one of the most beautiful parks I have visited. We climbed Gros Morne Mountain, an all-day hike to the top of a bald dome of rock where the elevation provides near-arctic climate and terrain. There, my companion nearly stepped on a ptarmigan whose summer mottling of gray and brown perfectly camouflaged the bird against a background of similar stones. The ptarmigan belongs to the partridge and grouse family. When winter comes, it exhibits one of nature's most incredible transformations, turning a pure, snowy white.

John Cabot is credited with the "discovery" of Newfoundland in 1497. This was a neat trick as the Vikings had already landed there about five hundred years earlier. And in fact, Portuguese, English, and Basque fishermen had been fishing the rich waters along the northeastern shores for some time. But we mustn't be too hard on Cabot—he'd really been looking for India, after all.

The mixture of peoples who are today all proud Newfoundlanders trace their ancestries back to the English, French, Portuguese, Basque, and Spanish. There is a distinct native accent still held by some that is nearly unintelligible to outsiders. I was once approached by a young Newfoundlander in the Halifax airport. He seemed to be asking me directions in what I vaguely recognized as English, but I was unable to decipher a single word of what he said. After a minute or two of my standing there with my mouth open, the fellow smiled broadly as though my reaction was a familiar one, shook my hand, and walked away.

The people of Newfoundland were among the most friendly and accommodating that I have come across anywhere. That welcome, combined with their extraordinary island, is enough to entice anyone back. One of these years, I am going to acquiesce to my partner's annual plea. And, trust me, we will take the kayaks.

A Lobster under Every Rock

When I was a boy, I would go down to the wharf in the little Nova Scotian cove where my father spent his boyhood summers and watch the fishermen come in. It was a singular experience.

Half-a-dozen small boats worked from the local wharf. They went to sea at three or four in the morning and were usually back by one in the afternoon, their holds loaded down with mackerel, herring, haddock, halibut, and the ubiquitous cod, backbone of the maritime fishery. From our porch, I could hear the seagulls cry as they followed the boats in for their accustomed treats as the fish were cleaned. My grandmother would send me down to purchase a codfish head, which she then boiled up with a large plate of potatoes for dinner. Cod is one of the more bland-tasting denizens of the deep, but this fish was fresh. It always tasted good, although I could never bring myself to try the eyeballs, a real delicacy. Still, there was plenty to eat. The head of a large cod can easily be the size of a basketball. I never became completely used to the sight of that enormous head—as large as my own—staring at me from a platter surrounded by new potatoes.

Down at the wharf, I watched the men haul hundreds of fish from the holds and expertly clean them with a few quick strokes of the cleaning knife. Then they doused the fish a few times with seawater and tossed them into huge barrels layered with salt. That was how salt cod made its way to market. The fishermen were always willing to sell directly from the wharf in those days.

About twenty years ago, everything changed when the unions took over the canneries. Now fishermen are forced to sell all their produce directly to the factories, without exception. But by that time,

the great fisheries offshore were nearing depletion anyway. The arrival of the big floating cannery ships, often hailing from Europe and
Japan, caused severe overfishing of the large banks south of Newfoundland and even of the smaller banks off Nova Scotia.

Throughout the sixties and seventies, I watched the death of this
small fishing industry. It was much the same as the death of the small
farming operations that occurred in the 1980s. By the end of the
1970s, if there were any boats going out at all from our local wharf,
they would struggle back late in the day with perhaps half-a-dozen
cod in the hold. The herring, haddock, and halibut were virtually
gone from the range of these small-boat, traditional fishermen.

Today, only a few sport or subsistence fishermen leave from the
local wharf. To purchase fish for which I once ran a few hundred feet,
we must now drive thirty miles to the local cannery, where we can
only buy frozen fish, as the bulk of the catch is frozen instantly while
still far at sea.

Shellfish have also fallen on hard times. My father likes to tell the
story of when he was a boy and his mother would send him off secretly to the shore to get some lobster for dinner. They were under
every rock, and in a few minutes he could collect a dozen or more.
The secrecy part was because his mother didn't want the neighbors to
know that they were so poor they had to eat lobster. When the local
minister or schoolteacher came to dinner, they were always given the
real delicacy, salt pork.

Lobsters are much harder to come by now, although they have
rebounded somewhat from serious depletions a few years ago. Today,
they are nearly always raised in pounds and are quite uniformly one
to two pounds in weight. The giants of years ago are gone. Other
shellfish have undergone periodic scares from a variety of contaminants. A regular trip to dig our own clams was a tradition in our
family for decades. We do it much less often now and only after
checking with the authorities to be sure there are no warnings out.
Shellfish are filter-feeders and can accumulate large amounts of relatively low-level contaminants simply because so much of the sub-
stance will pass through their bodies as they feed. As a result,
shellfish often contain lead, chromium, arsenic, and cadmium. Finfish
will also accumulate chemicals like PCBs from the water passing
through their gills and skin.

Yet fish from the ocean are still considered a safer bet than fresh-water fish, which have to put up with man's pollution in far greater amounts. Small fish are safer to eat than larger ones, and it is always advisable to discard the innards and all visible fat. Cooking on a grill allowing the fat to drip away also helps eliminate toxins.

It is a different world today, one where small fishermen can't survive and where fish fanciers must question their dinner's origins—one where the smallest fish are the safest, and where pregnant women are advised to avoid contaminated sportfish.

I still walk down to that wharf and stare into the waters where I once caught eel for supper. I don't see any eel anymore by our wharf. I'm not terribly surprised.

The Oldest Fur Trader

The room was large and bright with bay windows that looked out on the huge old chestnut tree. It was the light coming through those windows that I remember so clearly forty years later; a vaporish, hazy sort of light. It was filled with particles of dust that drifted slowly, hypnotically upward on the long beams of yellow, disappearing suddenly through the windows as though they had passed into another dimension.

The room was spare. There were hardwood floors, aging lace curtains, an enormous desk by the bay window. The rolltop was stuck three-quarters of the way open and had been that way as long as I had known it, the desktop piled with papers.

Everywhere in that room, piled on the floor, on the desk, on the windowseat that ran along the bay window, were stacks of animal hides and furs. Bound with plain white string in batches of ten or fifteen were columns of brown and pale mink; fall, winter, and spring muskrat; white weasel; dark and gray raccoon; short, long, and broad stripe skunk; silvery and reddish wildcat; fisher; lynx; otter; and, of course, the red and silver cross foxes.

Sitting at that desk, my grandfather ran his business. A fur trader who worked out of his home in Amherst, Nova Scotia, he called this place "Scotia's Reliable Fur House."

Prices have changed. His circular for the 1938–39 season listed a large, dark mink for fifteen dollars, a lynx for just twenty-eight dollars, and the silver cross fox was forty dollars.

For years, he had hunted and trapped by himself using an enormous old musket and piles of leg-traps that still turned up in the attic

The oldest fur trader in Canada, Edgar Ivy Angus.

and cellar of the old Victorian home during my childhood explorations of the 1950s. My father remembers his dad staggering into the kitchen on a cold winter's night bent under the weight of a huge stack of furs. He would release the load with a groan and stand before the fire, face beet red, lungs heaving from exhaustion, and wait for the warmth to penetrate his limbs.

Then Granddad woke up one day and realized that it would be one hell of a lot easier to sit at home and have others bring the furs to him. From the moment of that revelation, he became a fur trader, traveling every year to the traders and trappers convention in Montreal until well into his nineties. When he finally retired, a special ceremony was thrown for him as the oldest active fur trader in Canada.

For a boy of eight or ten, this was all pretty heady stuff. None of my friends had such a fascinating place to go, rooms filled to the ceiling with dead things—oh, glorious! The house seemed alive with death. In the parlor was an enormous bearskin, shot by that musket, the head still attached, teeth beared—so to speak. Upstairs, down the narrow, dark hallway, was my grandfather's bedroom. He had no blankets on his bed, only a single, enormous and incredibly soft cover made of lynx. The secret goal of each of my visits was to sneak into that room and lie on the lynx.

They're all gone now, the stacks of fur, the colorful characters, often Indians, who delivered them, the old rolltop sold, the musket stolen, the Victorian home converted to low-income housing, my grandfather dead. But in my mind, I can see him still, poring over the huge ledgers in which he entered each transaction in meticulous longhand, his aging fingers growing slower as the years passed, the business itself slowing down until in his nineties only a few loyal customers remained. But still he made the long train trip to Montreal because it was what he had done for the better part of a century.

It was a way of life that had emerged more than four hundred years earlier when a French navigator by the name of Jacques Cartier, failing to find the Northwest Passage he had sought, instead turned his efforts to trading with the Indians. The beaver pelts he took back to Europe became a sensation.

It was a way of life based on the natural bounty of the land; a cruel life, with no mercy for the creatures of the wild. If he ever thought about that, and I doubt that he did, my grandfather would likely have said that the creatures were put there by God for man to use. They were a gift. And so something noble was made out of what was certainly one of the most bloody of pastimes.

Yet the old man was the most gentle, soft-spoken, and kindly soul that I have ever known. He never raised his voice, a reaction, perhaps, to my grandmother's, which was forever elevated in its own penetrating soprano. That stentorian peal could reach the farthest corners of the old house and had belted forth "Rock of Ages" at countless funerals.

For years, Grandfather cultivated a growing deafness that enabled him to ignore "Mother's" clarion call. More than once, I had observed him perk his head up when she began to sound her hail, and instantly the old fellow was up and climbing the staircase to the third floor, which was his private realm and where she never went.

It was not so much that they didn't get along, but that he was of an entirely different nature, a placid, quiet, contemplative man who eschewed confrontation of any kind. When not poring over his ledgers, he would prefer to sit in the parlor and read John the Apostle or play that same "Rock of Ages" on the piano, a sound that took on surreal dimensions, for the old upright had not been tuned in thirty years. I can still bring forth an accurate memory of that racket, a melodic din unlike any other on God's earth, a rendering that seemed to exist in all keys at once—a tone-deaf gathering of angels.

My only religious exposure came from my grandparents. Whenever they came to visit in New York, my grandmother would whisk me off to church against my father's muttered protests, for he had absorbed none of their feelings in this area. And when we went to stay at the aging and falling-down family home on Nova Scotia's Eastern Shore, Granddad's one and only rule was a gathering each evening in the parlor.

Here, he would sit in a molding armchair—everything molded in that house, without heat and closed eleven months of the year against the foggy maritime weather. Here, he would put his flimsy wire spectacles on, lean close in under the dim yellow light and read from John the Apostle in a voice that was both compelling and soothing.

As a boy of nine or ten, I grew fond of those readings, not for their content, but for the stark nature of the gathering; all the family assembled in that crumbling house in a damp meadow deep in the North Woods, Granddad's words punctuated by the distant and mournful moan of the foghorn at the harbor entrance.

After the reading, I would step outside into the darkness and stare up in awe at a sky burgeoning with stars. Here was a blackness unlike any I had known. Leaping from horizon to horizon, the Milky Way sliced through it like all bottomless eternity, and if ever there was a moment for me to *believe*, it was then.

Only once did I ever see Granddad in a moment of weakness. At the age of ninety, he would still take an old berry pot and head off alone across the bogs that stretched for miles through the North Woods. Never, in almost a century of picking bakeapples, had his sense of direction deserted him.

But the inevitable finally happened. Somehow, he became disoriented. He wandered for hours, beating occasionally on his pot to signal his whereabouts. Eventually, the whole family was out looking for him, including myself. I shall never forget the look of embarrassment and bewilderment when we found him at last. He never picked berries again.

Still, his independence never quite left him. A year before his death, a nephew who kept an eye on the old fellow happened to drive by the large, old home in Amherst during a winter snowstorm. There, atop a long ladder, was my grandfather, fussing with something at the top of the chimney. Horrified, but afraid to distract him, the nephew sat in his car, his heart in his mouth, until Granddad finally made his way down.

Granddad was ninety-four when he died. I was just eighteen. A man of eighty before my earliest memories of him, he had already witnessed most of a century before I was born. He had been a young schoolteacher while Queen Victoria still reigned, a father to my father before the first World War—the Great War. When I began to contemplate my first adult job, he had been in the work force for seventy-eight years.

That's experience.

And I learned from it—from him. His character was that of a man fully at peace with himself. Gentle, compassionate, a loving grandfather, yet also a man who was not afraid to question the world. When, in his nineties, the local clergyman began to preach hellfire and brimstone, my grandfather would have none of it. He believed in a God who was loving and forgiving. There was no room for hellfire. He stopped going to church after ninety faithful years.

Still, I like to think God looked kindly upon my grandfather. I like to think Granddad would be pleased that his grandson now plies the frigid coastal waters of his homeland in the ancient way, in a kayak. He lived a long and fulfilled life. A life of quiet dignity.

The oldest fur trader in Canada.